Call Centers Made Easy

How to Build, Operate, and Profit from Your Small Business Call Center

by

Stephen Medcroft

Aegis Publishing Group, Ltd.
796 Aquidneck Avenue
Newport, Rhode Island
401-849-4200
www.aegisbooks.com

Library of Congress Catalog Card Number: 2001033389

Aegis Publishing Group, Ltd.
796 Aquidneck Avenue
Newport, RI 02842

International Standard Book Number: 1-890154-45-8

Printed in the United States of America.

10 9 8 7 6 5 4 3 2 1

Library of Congress Cataloging-In-Publication Data:

Medcroft, Stephen, 1967-
     Call centers made easy : how to build, operate, and profit from your small business call center / Stephen Medcroft
     p. cm.
     Includes index.
     ISBN 1-890154-45-8
     1. Call centers. 2. Small business—Management. I. Title

HE8788 .M43 2001
658.8'12—dc21

2001033389

Acknowledgments

Thank you to my wife, Keli, for your encouragement, understanding, and input. Your support has allowed me to stretch myself beyond all my previous achievements to reach for ever greater success in our life. A big thank you also to our children—Destiny, Gabrielle, and Cairo—who have patiently put up with the seemingly countless hours I spent locked away in my room while working on this book.

Thank you to John McMahon, Jake Petersen, David White, and Ron Thompson for reading sections of this book and providing me with the kind of valuable feedback that helped to make it something I am proud of.

Thank you to Bob Mastin, my publisher, for first listening to my idea and then overseeing its transformation into a book. I look forward to a long and productive relationship with you. I'd also like to thank Dee Lanoue, my editor, for helping to make this book much stronger and more readable.

Finally, thank you to everyone who has been part of my career in telecommunications. If you have ever been my employer, colleague, customer, consultant, friend, or supporter—I thank you.

Contents

Introduction

. . . .

ON FIRST IMPRESSION, the call center that I was invited to tour brought to mind the atmosphere of a classified military installation. A large foyer, capable of holding 50 or more, was bounded on the far side by a long, curving desk that effectively barred any unauthorized entry to the rooms beyond. And, though the wall behind the desk was glass, nothing could be seen from the foyer. A clever architect had angled the walls so that the bulk of the interior remained safely hidden.

In addition to being issued a special badge, visitors were required to have an escort while in the building. So, I signed my name to receive my badge and sat back to wait for my escort.

As I waited, it became clear to me that whatever went on in this building was protected by a high level of security. Employees came and went through what appeared to be an impenetrable double-glass revolving door. To access this door, they first swiped a card across a reader; but only after a green light flashed and a chime acknowledged them were they spun through. It seemed to me that many of them threw a cautious glance over their shoulders as they passed back and forth. I imagined that they must be constantly aware of the watchful eye of security.

My escort arrived to claim me, and now it was my turn to pass through the spinning glass door. As we entered the interior of the building, my impression of a military installation quickly gave way to that of a college classroom. I smelled paint and drywall and industrial-grade carpet.

I could hear the call center before I saw it, and it wasn't what I had expected. I had envisioned a maddening crush of competing conversations as each speaker attempted to make his sales pitch to the party on the other end of the line. But it was much more controlled than that. The sound I heard was more of a hum, a purposeful hum. Soon we turned a corner—and there it was.

"This was the first stadium we put up," my guide said. Stadium? Yes, I could see what he meant. We stood on a walkway about 15 feet wide that ran around the perimeter of the room. The ceiling, 25 feet above us, was festooned with banners proclaiming the achievements of outstanding employees, while monitors mounted high up on the walls flashed numbers down to the throng of workers below.

Following my eyes, my guide explained: "The monitor displays let the sales groups know how the center is performing. They tell us what the statistics are at the moment, how they've stacked up over the last hour, and how this stadium compares to the other two."

"The other two?" I asked.

"Oh, yeah. This was the first; now there are three. One takes all the incoming calls. Another makes a lot of outgoing calls—sales calls, follow-ups—that kind of thing. The third is split up depending on what kind of calls we need most."

Thirty feet below us, descending tiers of office cubicles housed some 175 call center operators and supervisors. From each walled cube of floor space, employees conducted their business, while runners and agents moved back and forth along the aisles that diagonally traversed the stadium.

All this was Insight.com, a deliverer of computers, computer parts, software, and accessories. In all, Insight.com employed about 500 people on the telephone plus an entire support staff. I couldn't help but wonder what Alexander Graham Bell would think if he could see this application of his invention.

Do you think he ever dreamed that the telephone would become such an important tool that entire businesses would be based upon it? Do you think he could have foreseen the day that the use of his device would be so commonplace that neither you nor I can imagine being without a telephone? Could he have imagined workers sitting in front of terminal displays, all the tools of their trade within arm's reach, whose only purpose is to talk with every caller delivered to them by a huge telephone machine?

My tour continued through the two other stadiums and ended in the computer room. Here, rows of aluminum racks seven feet tall held huge and powerful computers—the Insight.com Web servers and the internal software that supported the business. Independent of the racks was the phone system itself, which consisted of baby blue towers softly pitching the purr of their cooling fans throughout the room.

"That's it," said my guide.

We talked for a little while longer about what each box did and what it processed. Some boxes were responsible for moving the tens of thousands of calls per day that the center handled; others provided the necessary connections to the public telephone network for bringing those calls to the center. Because every incoming call represents an opportunity for an Insight.com agent to earn business, a special call distribution system is used to assign the calls equitably among all the operators.

One software program answered all sales calls automatically and, via recordings, asked the callers to wait for an agent to come on the line. Other servers and software recorded all calls for the quality assurance team. By using this record of live calls, an agent's work could be spot-checked easily. Naturally, there was a voice mail system, and yet another system analyzed Insight.com's ability to capture and serve customers as they called in with their questions and requests.

All together, the clean, static-free room with bright lights and white tiled floor represented several million dollars worth of technology, not to mention thousands of hours of thought, preparation, and research implementation. And all of it was necessary. Every box could be justified as a sound investment for Insight.com.

What Is a Call Center?

Do you have a call center within your business? Ask Insight.com and the answer is obviously yes, but for many businesses the answer is not so clear. Let me propose a working definition of a call center: A call center is any business, or group within a business, that has primary contact with customers or vendors over the telephone.

With this definition in mind, we see that a sales desk at an auto parts store or a reservations desk at a hotel are both call centers. Ticket booths, an appointment scheduler for a doctor's office, and even a team of executive assistants (fielding calls and confirming their boss's appointments) could be considered call centers. Likewise, a sales support team for reps in the field or a technical support line for your customers each comprises a call center. In some call centers, a group of people handles the calls, but in other centers, there may be only one person.

A telephone call between you and a customer or vendor is an opportunity to form and encourage a business relationship. In fact, for many of us today, telephoning is the primary way we maintain ongoing relationships in business. For companies such as Insight.com, the telephone may be the only direct, human-to-human contact their customers will have.

Even when we can see our customers face to face, the telephone still plays a major role. The truth is, our telephones are probably the most cost-effective and efficient tools we have to grease the wheels of commerce. If you can manage that phone call well, you have likely gained a customer. Poorly managed calls only waste the opportunities you had to do business.

To take advantage of the calls that come your way, always extend a courteous and professional manner, speak well, and communicate clearly. For help on doing just that, I recommend you read *1-800-Courtesy—Connecting With a Winning Telephone Image* by Terry Wildemann (Aegis, 1998).

Though the human aspect of a telephone connection is certainly important, what about the physical aspect, the technological side? That's where this book comes in. In these pages, I intend to help you answer your calls in an appropriate manner and time frame, flow calls in and out of your business effectively, and share sales calls among your employees. I can help you provide unfettered dial tone access for those who are chasing business on your behalf, and I can help you track and measure the efforts your business makes on the telephone accurately.

If this kind of help and information sounds good to you, read on.

HOW THIS BOOK WILL HELP YOU

What do you do for a living? What is your first order of business when you arrive at your office or workplace? Who do you see on a daily basis in your business? What are you producing? What is your expertise?

For over ten years, a friend of mine has supplied packaging to the retail industry. You know what I mean—the little box the jeweler gave you for the ring you bought for your anniversary or the elegantly printed paper sack that the custom candle store sent your purchase home in. He can tell me about every size and shape of packaging for every purpose and need, plus every foil embossment or printing option that's available. By just listening to what kinds of products a retail store sells, he can come up with an inexpensive, classy, or creative package for customers to carry away their merchandise. If I ever need advice on product or retail packaging, he's my expert.

If you've been at your job for a while, I'm sure you've become an expert in your field, too. However, the fact that you are reading this book leads me to assume that you also devote at least part of your life to managing telecommunications for your business. In addition to your main area of expertise, you may already have a good understanding of how telecom products and services relate to your business. Do you know what a T1 line is or why you would have one? Are you familiar with the names of the parts you need to buy to increase the size of your phone system?

On the other hand, telecom may be a new world to you. You may feel overwhelmed by the multitude of unknown terms and acronyms you need to learn. Or you may feel harried by the companies that call you every day with offers of new and better telecom services or cheaper rates.

I like to think I am an expert of sorts. To convince you of that, let me outline what I have been doing these many years.

I started out as a telephone operator and eventually learned enough about the equipment I used every day to become the office expert. The company I worked for grew, and soon I was asked to manage the phone system full time. It was my responsibility to fix all the little problems that seemed to occur on a daily basis—the faulty telephones or the handsets that went bad. In addition, I chased down complaints about staticky lines or features that wouldn't work.

By acquiring a deep understanding of this one system, I was able to save my company the expense of hiring a vendor to resolve every minor issue. Later, when auditing the company's long-distance telephone bills, I learned how to reorganize our carrier's services, thus saving my company even more money. All in all, my tenure at this company was a wonderful three-year education in telecom.

Next I ventured off into the selling world. I clearly remember how nerve-racking that first meeting with a real customer was.

I couldn't get over the discomfort of attempting to sell a $10,000 phone system—not because the price was too high for the product, but because $10,000 seemed like so much money to me! I remember that the meeting went well, however, due to the fact that I was on comfortable ground when talking about the technology. It was the subject I knew best.

That first opportunity set the foundation for my sales career. I have continued to grow and to learn while watching significant milestones pass: a $25,000 sale; my first $75,000 sale; followed by $100,000, $500,000, and $800,000 single sales. Soon, I was considered a top salesperson, and the manufacturers of the equipment I sold recognized my successes.

In addition to selling, I have also designed and implemented scores of PBX and telephone systems. I have researched and packaged all varieties of peripheral systems, such as voice mail systems and call tracking software programs. I also spent a chunk of time managing the statewide operations of a $125 million long-distance carrier in Arizona.

My love of computers led me to specialize in the integration of computers and telephone systems. In this area, I have outfitted businesses with products such as those that place voice mail messages in an email inbox, and technologies such as screen pops, where a customer's record pops up on an agent's computer desktop at the same time that the telephone call comes in.

There have been numerous opportunities to learn—seminars and classes on call center applications and Novell system administration, a certification class in unified messaging installation, plus books and industry emails that discuss call center technology and telephony in general.

As an equipment, carrier, and data specialist, I have been challenged to solve a wide variety of telecommunications problems, and this career has given me great satisfaction, constant change, and growth. It has also challenged me to stay sharp and current in my field. In my newest role as a telecom writer, it is my sincere wish to distill these many experiences and pass the knowledge I now possess to you.

What this book is meant to be

This book is structured so that if you venture into an area you are already familiar with, you can easily skip ahead. For the reader who wants to move gradually from basic to advanced concepts, this book will feed you the information you need in a logical way. Regardless of your level of experience, I promise that you will gain a better grasp of the terms and technologies peculiar to telecommunications. Lastly, hang on to this book! You'll find it a reliable resource whenever you need to brush up on certain technologies and their use in the future.

I like to think that you are reading this book because you have a call center within your business. Or perhaps you use the telephone as a primary point of contact with your customers and vendors, and you want to take advantage of any technology that allows you to improve your business. Ideally, your work might be to advise businesses on their telecommunications needs. If so, nothing would give me greater satisfaction than seeing you learn and grow through the words captured herein.

What this book is *not* meant to be

Though it saddens me to say it, I do believe that the telecom field is the single most jargon- and acronym-laden industry out there. Indeed, 99 percent of the thousands of terms, phrases, and acronyms tossed around in the telecom world are most likely irrelevant to your purposes. You certainly don't need to memorize acronyms in order to use telecommunications technology to improve your business.

Nonetheless, I have included a glossary of terms in this book. It is by no means comprehensive, though, because I didn't see the need to repeat the exhaustive efforts of such resources as Harry Newton's *Telecom Dictionary* or the *Telecom & Networking Glossary* from Aegis Publishing Group.

Nor is this book meant to be a buying guide to call center technology in specific terms. That means you will not read brand names, unless specifically relevant, or be told where a particular solution is available. Your market for call center technology is in your yellow pages, in your neighborhood, or with the telecom equipment suppliers active in your area. There are far too many excellent companies that specialize in the problems of handling telephone traffic to single out only one or two.

At the end of this book you will find two appendices. One lists publications that address issues relating to call centers, and the other lists organizations that serve call centers.

WHO ARE YOUR CUSTOMERS?

First off, let's agree to use the term "customer" to mean the people who are in contact with your business, regardless of whether you call them or they call you. Your customers may be purchasers of your products or services, or they may be suppliers and vendors to your business or department.

Next, let's go back to the question I started this section with: Who are your customers? Whoever they are, the calls they make to your place of business are of utmost importance to you. Therefore, your ability to stay in contact with them is also vitally important.

Most likely, you give out a telephone number or two for customers to use to call your business, and there are rules in place on how those calls are answered. Do you have a receptionist or other person whose main duty is to answer the calls? Are calls answered within three rings? Five rings? Then what? Are calls subsequently transferred to someone who will respond to the caller's needs? Do you have a voice mail system that answers calls? Does your voice mail give your callers the option to direct themselves (by pressing numbers on their telephone's Touch-Tone keypad)?

Conversely, are you the one calling customers? Do you have a quota of customers you need to reach in an hour? Twenty? Fifty? No matter how you have arranged for telephone calls to be handled within your business, your objective is to increase your ability to connect profitably with your customer, right?

You already know that more calls and better calls translate into more and better business. Call center technologies can help you reach these business goals and bring you success beyond what is possible without them. These technologies will both enhance the caller's experience and improve your productivity, which is exactly what you want.

When attempting to identify your customer, we're not talking about general business traffic, the day-to-day phone calls that fly back and forth across the telephone network for any number of reasons. We're talking about the meat-and-potatoes calls that relate to the business of your company or department.

If you supply the materials that municipal governments use to make road signs, your customers are the callers who are placing orders, checking prices, requesting catalogs, and asking about specific sizes of signs or anchors or posts. If you are a small distributor of a one-of-a-kind automotive accessory, you may spend all day trying to reach as many of your customers as you can—the managers of auto parts shops, body shops, repair shops, and retail chains. Maybe your company uses 50 different types of software applications, and you are part of an in-house technical support team. Your customers are the company's employees all across the country who are calling with questions concerning the software they are using.

Now that you've identified your customers, let's examine how they contact you and how you can ensure that contact is the best experience you can offer. Throughout this book I have included short histories of various businesses that use call center technologies in many different ways. Some of the names have been fictionalized out of respect to that business's privacy, but the examples are real.

As you read about the problems and experiences of these enterprises, no doubt you will see parallels and similarities to your own business. My goal is to show you how call center technology solved these problems, and how similar solutions could be applied in your own company.

If you begin to read unfamiliar terms, don't panic. In the pages that follow, I have taken great pains to slice the various technologies into easily digestible chunks. By the time you reach the end of this book, you'll be comfortable enough to choose the right technology for improving your business.

Once you know who your customer is, you'll be able to see where the call center is within your business. It may not have been obvious to you. You'll also see who the people are that make up your call center staff. Does your company's call center consist of just one person, or everyone, or a particular group within your business?

The most important aspect of any call center, of course, is the people who staff it. At its core, a call center is nothing more than a group of working people. It includes the agents who man the front lines and talk to the callers, the supervisors who make the day-by-day choices on how business will be conducted, and the managers who decide what the overall mission of the call center is. These are the folks you depend on, and you can help them work as productively as possible by taking full advantage of the sophisticated tools available today.

So, let's roll up our sleeves and dig into the technology that has helped millions of businesses grow bigger, stronger, and wealthier through their call centers. Are you ready?

Section 1

Background and Basics

Chapter

1

Phone Systems

. . . .

IN THE PAGES AHEAD, we are going to focus on the many ways different call center technologies are used. Most of these technologies are specific, customized tools designed to help you achieve a particular goal. Examples include predictive dialers, which allow outbound call centers to greatly increase the number of calls an agent can make per hour; or automatic call distribution systems, which stack and rack incoming callers and then dish them out evenly to a group of agents.

As you read about the many different boxes you can install and the various software programs you'll need to learn, you may wonder why any of it is necessary. You've gotten along pretty well so far with the reliable old telephone service you already have. Why do you need anything else?

My answer is that today's call center technology can significantly improve what already exists. Don't get me wrong—business telephone systems are not stupid machines. In fact, I love the things. I've built a career around them, and I believe they are one of the most important investments any business will make.

More to the point, though, your phone system is the foundation on which your call center is built. To take advantage of the improvements modern call center technologies can afford you, it's important to thoroughly understand what you already have. Doing so will ensure that the technology choices you make are the right ones for your business.

Modern, high-tech business telephone systems are extremely sophisticated. Usually, they are based on a digital architecture much like your personal computer; they are reliable; and they offer software capable of driving dozens, even hundreds, of features and options.

The core purpose of a business telephone system is to give your employees shared access to the telecommunications resources of your company, such as telephone lines, voice mail systems, paging systems, and receptionists. Each employee takes advantage of this access via his or her individual phone set.

Broadly, there are three basic categories of business telephone systems: key, PBX, and hybrid. Let's look at each in turn.

KEY TELEPHONE SYSTEMS

The name "key system" usually refers to a smaller telephone system of, say, 32 phones or less. On these small systems, every phone line appears on every telephone set connected to the system.

A customer of mine is the U.S. representative for an Italian sandal manufacturer. This company uses eight main telephone lines, and there is a button to represent each line on every phone throughout the office. So, even though a receptionist is employed, the responsibility for answering calls can be shared by everyone in the office whenever that person isn't available.

Features on key systems have generally been limited, but today you will find many features available that were formerly the province of larger systems only. This happy fact is due to the flexibility of digital architecture. Also, most phone systems are simply proprietary computers running phone system software such as voice mail. For small offices, key systems deliver the benefits of a big office phone system at a fairly low entry price.

PBX TELEPHONE SYSTEMS

PBX is the acronym used for private branch exchange. Most likely, this will mean nothing to you until you read the story that follows.

When phones were a relatively new and rare technology , the connections between telephones were accomplished manually by branch exchange operators. This is how it was done:

Courtesy of telecomwriting.com

A copper wire connected to your telephone set would wind its way along your neighborhood telephone poles to an operator board located in a telephone office. This office was called the central office, a term still used today. There, it would terminate at a panel, known as a cord board, where the operator (usually female) sat. On her board, she would see a light for every connection she was responsible for. To make cross connections between lines, she had to use plug-in patch cables, or cords—hence the name cord board. A single operator might handle 100 lines or so on her cord board.

If you wanted to make a call, you manually drove an electrical signal down the line by turning the hand crank attached to your telephone set. This signal alerted the operator to come on the line. She then manually patched your call to the line connecting the person you wanted to talk to. If you were calling outside your own exchange, she would patch the call to another operator board across interoffice lines, or trunk lines.

Now, if your company had enough telephones at its place of business to fill its own board, you would hire your own operator and—voila!—you had a private branch exchange. (It's neat the way a long-winded story all comes together, isn't it?)

Manually switching telephone calls was an expensive process, but branch exchange operators were the rule until the invention of automated central office switching systems. Though decidedly more advanced today, central office switches are still the way the public telephone network works.

For a private company, a PBX may be an economical alternative to paying the phone company for a separate line to every desk. Employee phones become internal extensions of a private system, and these internal lines are paid for only once. Also, because not every employee needs an outside line at the same time, a company can share a smaller number of connections to the outside world. For example, 10 phone lines might accommodate 50 employees with no problem. Thanks to the economies of scale and the huge price tags of these private systems, most of the developments in telephone technology have been made with the PBX system in mind.

HYBRID TELEPHONE SYSTEMS

Today's hybrid telephone systems are the direct result of both rapid improvement of the semiconductor processor plus the ability of digital-based systems to emulate features of the PBX (via software). These systems are appropriate for the markets requiring 30 or so phone lines up to 200 or more.

There are two forms of hybrid systems. The first is a scaled-down version of a PBX with most of the same capabilities and features intact, but with a limited maximum size and processing capacity. The second type of hybrid is a key system, where the manufacturer has enlarged a small system in order to take advantage of a faster processor. Previously, only a PBX could accommodate digital trunking lines (DID, T1), but most hybrids have that ability today.

Business telephones continue to evolve and become ever more sophisticated.

Courtesy of Toshiba America Information Systems, Inc.

Again, I would like to state that the business telephone system is a wonderful tool. As I describe and outline call center technologies in the sections that follow, you may realize that some of these capabilities already exist within your current telephone system. Wouldn't it be great to know that all you need is a minor tweak to your current system to reap all the benefits large call centers enjoy?

Chapter

2

Improving Your Business Telephone System

. . . .

WHEN COMPARED TO THE PLAIN old telephone on your desk, it's a fact that call center technologies and tools can decidedly improve business communications. Think for a moment about what's going on in your business.

Perhaps you are experiencing increased call volume, but don't want to hire extra employees just yet. Or perhaps you'd like to drive more sales calls. There are many good reasons for making improvements to your existing phone system, but regardless of your motivation and the technology you choose, the bottom line is the price tag. How do we justify the cost of such upgrades?

To start, let's examine why you are considering upgrades to your current phone system. Then, once you've determined how your business can profit from such changes, you can assign a value to them. I believe that your reasons for wanting to implement call center technology will generally fall into three categories.

CUSTOMER EXPERIENCE
In the first category, your reasons will involve somehow improving the experience your customer has when calling your

company. This was the case for the classified advertising department at *Seattle This Week*, a small local newspaper.

The ad department employed three agents to take orders, but if all agents were busy, what then? Previously, an agent would have to put his current caller on hold to answer an incoming call, then go back to the first caller to finish taking the order. If yet other calls came in, the agent would have to put each one on hold, returning to them later in the sequence he best remembered.

On the other side, customers might suffer a dozen interruptions just trying to place one ad order or be forced to wait for long periods if the agent forgot which call came in first. It's easy to see how frustration and miscommunication plagued both agents and customers. How much business was lost as a result?

The newspaper remedied this situation by implementing technology that automatically answered the phone when all agents were busy and queued the calls. In addition, the new system played recorded messages intermittently to let callers know they were still on hold and hadn't been forgotten. The messages assured customers that their business was important to the paper, thanked them for waiting, and asked them to continue holding for the next available agent.

Callers were also offered the option of leaving their number for a callback rather than continuing to hold. I'm sure you've heard these kinds of messages yourself. Lastly, a timer monitored holding time, and callers on hold for more than three minutes would be transferred directly to the department's manager.

Call center technology greatly reduced the confusion the newspaper's customers had experienced by giving them choices.

It allowed them to decide whether to hold or hang up, and it even entertained them if they chose to hold. Being queued was infinitely preferable to the old alternative.

PRODUCTIVITY

In the second category, your goals for upgrading your system center around tangibly increasing the productivity of your agents. After *Seattle This Week*'s ad department installed its new phone system, greater productivity proved to be an added bonus. Because the phone now rang only when an agent was free, agents could conclude one transaction before being forced into another. This meant they could also take the extra time to "up sell" and deliver better service. Other tangible benefits were noticed as well, such as fewer errors and decreased tension, which was attributed to the reduced noise level in the room.

Productivity was an important issue for an outbound market research company here in Phoenix. News and political organizations hire this company to canvass large geographical areas by telephone and ask popular opinion questions. Working from a list and dialing manually, agents had traditionally waded through a veritable sea of nonconnections—busy signals, unanswered ringing, and hang-ups.

Taking into account the time spent resting for a moment before dialing out or finishing the latest cup of company-supplied coffee, statistics showed that these agents were talking on the phone less than 18 minutes of every working hour. If we factor in salary and overhead for 30 agents, plus associated toll call charges, it's obvious there was a serious and costly lack of productivity.

This company decided on a call center technology that continuously dialed two phone numbers for every agent on duty, thus making dozens of attempted calls each minute. In addition, the system was able to monitor the line for an answer, distinguish between an answering machine and a live voice, and connect only valid "human" calls to the waiting agents. By mass dialing and filtering, these systems can keep agents on good calls for up to 54 minutes per hour.

MANAGEMENT

The third category of justifiable goals for implementing modern technology involves management. Will business be significantly improved so that management can see an impact on the bottom line? Will management have access to useful, accurate information on callers and employees, so necessary for decision-making and adapting to changing markets and customer demands?

Later in this book, you'll read about Greer Millwork, a Seattle-based wholesale distributor and installer of doors, related parts, and hardware. By adding two different reporting packages to its phone system, this company was able to measure the performance of its salespeople in ways other than simply sales numbers. The reports highlighted the fact that reps with low sales numbers made or took fewer calls than their peers and spent less (or too much) time on the phone with their customers. Such information helped this business to make needed changes.

You'll also read how American Consumer Debt Services, a non-profit credit counseling service, implemented a call reporting system for its call center with surprising results. After only a few days, several agents had to be fired for a bad habit of circumventing the system and ultimately stealing their salaries. This is what happened.

When reviewing the new reports, the system administrator noticed a high incidence of phone calls to the same long-distance phone number. It seems that one loyal employee liked to dial the automated information line of an out-of-state driver's license bureau. He would then hang on the line and listen to the lengthy, and no doubt helpful, driver information prompts, all the while pretending to be at work for his employer.

Other enterprising agents called their own extensions through the company's main telephone number. Once connected, they promptly placed themselves on hold and lived the dream of being a paid actor—that is, taking a salary for the role of doing a job. Could this type of abuse exist in your business?

As we discuss each technology in the following pages, think of how it relates to your business and how it can achieve each or all of the goals we've discussed. I'm sure that once you understand the effect that a given technology can have on your business, you will have no trouble justifying its price tag.

DETERMINING YOUR CALLER'S EXPERIENCE

One day, while visiting a customer of mine in Bellevue, Washington, I had a revelation. We had been talking about the goals he had for his call center. What did he want technology to do for him? How was it going to better his business?

This customer was in the business of developing software, and, as such, one of its natural call centers was the technical support department, or help line. Like most software companies, technical assistance could be reached via a toll-free number, but sometimes hard-to-resolve individual calls might tie up the line for hours. Worse, other callers might be waiting for an extended time just to ask a question that had a 10-second answer—and all on the company's dime.

It didn't take long for this company to be buried in phone call charges, and the helpless tech support staff routinely suffered the anger and frustration of irate callers, who had lost all patience during their sometimes lengthy wait. Clearly, this company wanted (and needed!) a different experience for both its callers and its employees.

My revelation was this: For any specifically inbound call center, you want to create the best possible experience for your callers so that the entire contact is slanted in your favor. Once you've determined the ideal caller experience for your business, you can then sit down and match the available technologies to that ideal.

Now, the above statements may not strike you as especially profound. But, too often, we focus on investigating and learning about all the various technologies out there, without knowing exactly what we want them to do for our businesses. That's backwards. There's no need to understand pulse code modulation or ground-start trunking or other technical folderol if you don't know what you want the technology to do for you.

To use call center technology wisely, you must know exactly how it can change your callers' experience when they dial your business. What do you want that experience to be? Try asking yourself the following questions:

- When do your customers call you?
- Why do they call you?
- What do you want them to hear when they call?
- What choices do you want them to have?
- What would you like them to hear while on hold?
- What is the maximum length of time they should be on hold?
- Is there a company you've called that uses a technology application you particularly like?
- In short, what is your idea of the perfect phone call?

If you think of your callers first, the question of which technologies to use in your call center can be answered easily. However, a much harder question comes next. How is your business going to pay for what you want?

JUSTIFYING CALL CENTER COSTS

We now see that a primary reason for businesses to build call centers is to provide a higher-quality customer experience. The right technology choices enable us to create that experience, but there must be a balance between the cost of the technology and its perceived benefit.

After many years of walking that tightrope with my customers, I have evolved a quasi-mathematical aid that I call the "help/annoy coefficient." It refers to a sliding scale, where, theoretically, the more technology you buy and employ, the better your customer's call experience will be.

At the upper end of the scale, you have the perfect call center—100 percent help, zero annoyance, and lots of expensive technology. At the low end, you have a single harried employee manually juggling a row of plain old telephones—minimal help, lots of annoyance, but little cash outlay. Somewhere on this scale is a help/annoy ratio you can live with at a dollar amount you can justify spending.

High-volume call concentration centers spend an incredible amount of money in overhead, but, somehow, there is always money available to pay for new technology. Indeed, call center designers can find money to pay for technology in ways that would surprise you.

How do they do it? The first rule is that every investment must pay for itself. More specifically, though, let me ask you the following:

Question: Why is so much effort spent in developing call center technology?

Answer: To reduce labor expense when staffing high-volume call concentration business units.

The bigger call centers usually process low-dollar transactions per call or a low percentage of sales per hundred calls. Many of them handle indirect revenue calls, such as technical support calls, follow-up calls, or billing questions. These types of calls don't make the centers any money per se, so unless your call center is processing $10,000 transactions one after the other, sales are not going to pay for the technology you want to buy. However, by using technology to enhance your agents' productivity and thus cut back on labor expense, significant savings can be realized. In fact, you could say that labor expense is the fabled mattress under which the money is hidden.

As an example, let's look at a call center here in Phoenix. It employs 120 agents at an average salary of $24,900 per year. If we bump that up to $38,000 each year to cover employees' benefits, insurance, and so on, this one company spends approximately $4,560,000 annually in raw labor costs.

The average agent at this center formerly answered 100 calls per day, staying with each caller about two minutes and thirty seconds. Technology was then introduced that automatically brought up the incoming caller's customer screen (known as a screen pop) before the agent answered the call. By eliminating that first fumble of questions needed to bring up the customer's account, 20 seconds were shaved off the average call.

Shorter average calls meant that the same number of calls could be handled by 10 percent fewer agents on the floor, which amounted to $456,000 savings in labor expense in only one year. Subsequently, this call center could afford to pump a half million dollars back into the business and pay for its investment in just one year.

That's a mind-boggling business reality, wouldn't you agree? Any payback under three years is seen as exceptional, yet this call center's investment was recouped by the second year!

In addition, we have not even touched on the extra dollars that were derived from happier customers, such as referrals, up-sells, and other opportunities, plus the recapture of business previously lost due to poor service. We can also factor in potential savings on telephone services. Shorter telephone calls certainly cost less, and fewer agents need fewer phone lines.

This particular call center instituted yet another technology that allowed callers to access their account information over the phone without going through an agent. In this way, some 15 to 30 percent of the company's calls will require no human interaction at all. No big deal, you say? Just another million dollars in labor savings per year!

The point to all this, of course, is to convince you that there's a ton of money to be tapped in labor and productivity savings. So, I'd like you to be cautious about judging a call center technology by its price tag. It would be a shame to have you rule out the perfect phone system for your business because you don't think you can afford to pay for it.

First take the time to add up your cost of doing business by telephone—labor, phone system, toll costs, and the hard costs associated with your product or service. Then, see where the new system will save money for you. I'm confident you'll find that creating a caller experience for your customers with a high-end help/annoy coefficient is well within your reach.

Chapter

3

Telephone Lines

THE WRITTEN WORD has been a reliable means of communication for thousands of years, and letter writing is still an affordable and effective method for contacting your customers. Today, however, there are many other communication methods available that take traditional letter writing one step further. For example, in the matter of a few minutes, we can use the phone lines to exchange pictures of our letters via a fax machine. That sure beats waiting for the post office to deliver our mail.

Email is another form of letter writing that has become so pervasive that many businesspeople I know can be reached faster over the Internet than by phone. Also, if you want your correspondence or advertising to reach an unlimited number of readers, simply post it on the World Wide Web. Businesses today often build a website for just that purpose.

Nonetheless, I believe telephone connections are the lifelines of commerce. You won't want to ignore the importance of other methods of communication, but if you've turned to this book as a resource, the telephone is clearly the mainstay of your business.

Have you ever been told to repeat something seven times in order to remember it? Or that an action needs to be repeated

21 days in a row for it to become a habit? Memory and habits may be improved by repetition, but to truly understand an idea, you must learn everything you can about the subject from its foundation on up.

The purpose of this book is to help you understand the inner workings of an automatic call distribution system. But to do that, I will also need to talk about how a telephone system works, how a line works, and how a toll-free number works. Otherwise, you wouldn't get the whole story.

Though selling and installing call center technology has been the focus of my career, I have held other jobs as well. At one point, I ran a branch office for a long-distance telephone company that provided services to call centers. Before that I was the computer network guy at a call center in Las Vegas, Nevada, and before that I was a shift supervisor at—you guessed it—a call center. In fact, my interest in call centers first began when I took a job at a friend's company processing credit card transactions on the graveyard shift.

At each of these jobs, I had the opportunity to learn and understand yet one more facet of the way call centers worked. No one progression in my career could have occurred without the base of knowledge that preceded it. How can you supervise a position you've never held? How can you support people on a system you've never worked with? How can you, as a salesperson, address the needs of a business you don't understand?

Keeping the above in mind, I intend the following sections to constitute a primer on the physical connection that allows you to communicate with your customers—your telephone service.

Some of you may already know this stuff, so let me remind you again to skip the parts you know or don't care about. You won't hurt my feelings, and, honestly, it is not my intention to bore you, tire you, or steal your precious free time. Most of all, I don't want to be responsible for a conversation with your kid that goes something like this: "I'm sorry, Timmy, I can't make your first T-ball game tonight because I have to read a section in this book about work. Even though it covers stuff I already know, the author insists on driving the most basic information down my throat over and over again because he once heard that you have to hear something seven times. . ."

Promise me that your kid comes first. However, if you aren't completely comfortable with all the wires that inhabit your telephone room or closet, read on. One warning—the acronyms can get kind of thick in here.

A BRIEF HISTORY OF THE TELECOM INDUSTRY

How many calls do you get each week from a salesperson offering the best service at the cheapest rates for both local phone lines and long distance? The deluge of offers we all receive nowadays is the direct result of government interventions that have freed up the telecommunications market. Today, any company that wants to go out on the pond to fish for your business is allowed to do so.

The public telephone network, which consists of the huge, spider-like run of wires and cables interconnecting almost every home and business in our country, began as a single business entity known as the Bell Telephone network. This network was conceived as a public utility, but it was also a regulated monopoly.

The rationale was that granting monopoly status would ensure telephone access for all of us because there would be no competition between enterprises. Therefore, if you happened to live in a hard-to-wire location miles from the center of town, the phone company's cost to bring service to you would be offset by the cost of servicing cheap-to-wire, high-density locations, such as business districts and city centers. By the 1970s, the network was pretty well built, and you could reach virtually any area in the country by telephone.

Then, as now, the phone company had two main revenue-producing businesses and one minor one. These businesses included your basic phone service, or connection to the public network, for which you received a monthly phone bill; long-distance service, for which you paid a metered per-minute rate for calls traveling over interstate telephone lines; plus the sales of various types of telephone equipment you might need to take advantage of the network. The government regulated how much these businesses could charge you in order to balance the phone company's profits against the public service it provided.

However, you can't stop progress, they say. Certain railroad and oil pipeline companies began to lay fiber-optic telephone lines in the ground along their rights of way, thus creating networks capable of carrying long-distance telephone and computer network traffic. With the availability of these independently owned networks, competitors appeared on the horizon, such as the upstart company that decided to build microwave radio towers for transmitting telephone calls between cities. Thus it happened that in 1969 Microwave Communications, Inc. (yes, MCI) began to compete directly with the Bell system for long-distance business.

Bell Telephone responded to the new competition with some creative and even illegal tactics. In some cases, customers were told that if non-Bell Telephone business equipment was connected to its network, the whole public telephone network would crash. Therefore, such telephone connections were expressly forbidden. In addition to this type of propaganda, Bell also used its ownership and control of the local telephone networks to block any competitor's access to long-distance customers.

This was the situation in 1983 when a federal judge, citing the Sherman antitrust laws, ruled that the Bell Telephone monopoly must be broken up. Known as the Divestiture Act of 1983, this judgment required Bell Telephone to divide its local service business into seven separate companies, called the regional Bell operating companies, or RBOCs—Ameritech, Bell Atlantic, BellSouth, Nynex, Pacific Bell, Southwestern Bell, and US West.

Nicknamed the "baby Bells," each RBOC was granted public utility status within predefined regional boundaries, or LATAs (local access transport areas). Each was also allowed to maintain the privilege of a limited monopoly in its market, but services and operations of any given RBOC were restricted to the LATA assigned to it by the Federal Communications Commission (FCC).

Telephone service between LATAs was reserved for the last chunk of the original Bell system, American Telephone & Telegraph (AT&T). Further, baby Bells were required to provide equal access to their networks for both customers and long-distance companies, including AT&T, thereby opening the floodgates for competition in the long-distance market. Today, we can choose among more than 300 companies for our long-distance telephone service.

Regardless of the headaches and hassles open competition seems to have brought with it, I would argue that the net results have been positive, especially for folks like you and me. As an example, it's interesting to note that a typical long-distance telephone call today costs a mere fraction of what it did before the Bell system's divestiture. I like that.

In 1996, those Washington whiz kids got together again and drafted the Telecom Reform Act. Their idea was that the existing barriers against competition in the local telephone business should be removed. Why? Well, it was no secret that the RBOCs and other local telephone companies were making plenty of money services they provided. Consider the literally billions of dollars we collectively spend each month on our telephone lines.

At a minimum, we each have one line, and many of us have a second line for the kids. Then, what about the extra line we put in so we can Web surf and not tie up our main line? And we can't forget the line that feeds our pager. Even the cell phones in our cars require a physical connection from the public telephone network to the radio cell site they communicate with.

Naturally, the local phone companies did not want to share this lucrative market, especially the RBOCs. They pointed out that they had invested huge sums of money in building their networks. Why should they take the risk of losing those investments to competitors? Besides which, they said, all those wanna-be local phone companies are free to compete for long-distance business, but we are restricted to our LATAs.

The FCC acknowledged these arguments to be reasonable, so an arrangement was made to satisfy both sides. Briefly, the local phone companies agreed to give competitors access to the networks they had built, and the FCC reciprocated by allowing the RBOCs to compete for long-distance business. Also, to ensure that the new CLECs (competitive local exchange carriers) could make a profit in the local service game, the FCC regulated how much existing local phone companies could charge to lease their network infrastructures.

Most likely, you have witnessed the results of this deal in your area. I know of at least 12 CLECs (pronounced "see-lecs") in

Phoenix alone. But, what all this upheaval really means to you and me is cheaper telephone service and the speedier availability of innovative telecom products.

With that history lesson behind us, let's get back to the business at hand—your call center. When your customers call into your business, they will use a variety of lines and services. Obviously, existing call centers already have their phone service in place, but if you are just setting up your center, your first decision must be: Which type of telephone service best meets the needs of my business? In the sections that follow, I'm going to help you answer that question.

CENTRAL OFFICE LINES

As a member of the telecommunications industry, I feel I am cursed. Almost every day, it seems, I have to add a new term to my mental glossary, most of them acronyms. Worse, this industry can't agree to use the same term for the same technology from one geographical region to another or even from one telecom field to another. So, I am apologizing in advance for the confusion in terms you are bound to come across.

As an example, we can use the subject of this section, the central office line. Sometimes it's called a CO (central office) line, so named for the neighborhood switching facility that connects individual lines to the rest of the network. At other times, it's called a 1FB, meaning one flat-rate business line, or a 1MB, for one measured business line. Yet other names include POTS (plain old telephone service) line and trunk line. It's easy to see how using so many names for the same item can confuse things.

Any of the above names, however, refer to the telephone line that is the basic building block of the telephone company's network. It provides service to your home, and most business telephone systems use it as well, only in greater quantities.

A CO line, our basic telephone line, consists of a single pair of copper wires twisted around one another and enclosed in some sort of sheath. This pair of twisted copper wires is the actual circuit through which electrical current flows—in on one wire and out on the other. Alexander Graham Bell performed various experiments with just such a circuit of twisted-pair copper wire. As we all know, his findings led to the invention of the analog telephone.

A good way to understand how a CO line works is to think about how your home phone works. First of all, a circuit must be closed for electrical current to flow through it. At home, the receiver on your idle telephone is actually depressing a switch that breaks the circuit. Ergo, no current. However, when you lift your receiver to make a call, the switch hook comes up and closes the circuit. The current that now begins to flow is called loop current. At your local central office, the switch recognizes that the circuit is closed and then sends dial tone down the line to indicate it is ready for instructions, that is, dialing.

Until recently, your instructions to a standard rotary telephone were conveyed by means of a method called dial-pulse signaling. In telecom lingo, a pulse refers to a change in the status of your line, or circuit, from closed (current is flowing) to open (current is absent). Each number on a rotary dial can be identified by that same number of pulses. For example, dialing the number "6" generates six pulses before the dial returns to its original position. Each digit of the phone number you want to call is transmitted to your central office switch in the same way.

You'll probably agree that the foregoing is interesting, but not too pertinent. There aren't many rotary phones used in business anymore. Nowadays, most telephones employ a push-button keypad for dialing and utilize a technology known as dual tone multifrequency (DTMF).

Dual Tone Multifrequency

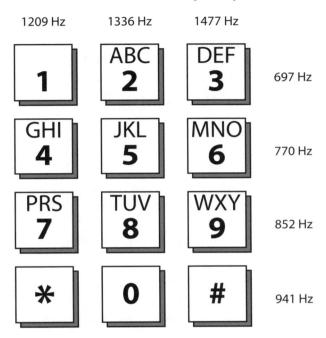

You and I are familiar with DTMF as Touch-Tone, which is an AT&T trademark. Touch-Tone signaling works by assigning a different tone to each vertical row and each horizontal row on your telephone's keypad. When you push a number or symbol, the tone you hear is actually a combination of the vertical and horizontal tones for that position. Thus, a unique tone is created for each of the twelve characters on your telephone's keypad. Other tones that you commonly hear on your telephone, such as busy signal, call waiting, or dial tone, are also unique combinations of tones.

Before going on to discuss other kinds of telephone lines, I would like to mention that there is a type of CO line known as a ground start trunk. In most respects, it functions in the same way as a regular CO line, but there is one difference. Instead of signaling the central office with an open loop current to start your phone call, this line is initiated by grounding the circuit. Certain types of telephone systems can only connect and disconnect reliably to the public telephone network by using grounding to signal the central office switch. So, you'll want to remember this tidbit of information.

To sum it all up, basic telephone service from your local phone company is provided over central office lines. However, when the needs of your business require more than basic service, the choices for telephone service can become somewhat complicated. Let's take a look now at some of the more sophisticated lines available today.

T1 SERVICE

If you choose T1 service, you will get a live, high-quality telephone circuit that runs 24 hours a day between your business and the phone company. These lines, also called T-span and DS1 lines, provide telephone service in a digital format. They can "speak" a specific protocol (that's a language in telecom talk), which both your phone equipment and the telephone company switching equipment use to communicate.

Think of when you make a dial-up connection to the Internet via your modem. Your computer grabs the modem; you hear dial tone on the line; and then you hear that familiar unintelligible squealing. If we had all the time in the world to listen, you and I could never decipher what is being said between the two machines. All we know is that they understand each other and that we can see or do what we want to see and do once the squealing stops.

A T1 line can carry 24 telephone calls all at the same time on a single connection. Twenty-four! One way to understand how this works is to think about the merry-go-round at your child's local playground. Pretend there are 24 kids riding it, and each one is sitting in exactly the same amount of space—one twenty-fourth of the merry-go-round. Now, imagine watching the ride as it goes around. If you kept your eyes staring straight ahead, each child would come into view for a fraction (one twenty-fourth!) of each revolution.

Essentially, that's how a T1 line can carry 24 calls. The total connection time of a single line is divided evenly into 24 perfectly synchronized slices. Then, devices on either end of the line—synchronized to the millisecond—use the narrow time window of each slice to pass a stream of digital information. In this way, each of the 24 time slices operates as one channel, or one regular telephone line's worth of information. The technical term for this process is time-division multiplexing (TDM).

What is digital signaling?

As I mentioned earlier, T1 lines use digital signaling, just like your computer. And we all understand those ones and zeros, right? Not me. When clients asked me why it mattered if this or that was digital, I had a tough time answering them. I could only define digital signaling in terms of results, such as cleaner lines or static-free lines. However, Herb Rosen, owner of Trans-West Telephone Company in Phoenix, Arizona, was able to help me out. He has long forgotten who first passed along this explanation to him, but we thank you whoever you are. I really think it's the best one I've heard. Now, get ready to use your imagination one more time.

Visualize that you have baked a cake at home in your California kitchen. It's a beauty to look at, and it may just be the greatest cake ever made. But if you put it in the back seat of your car and drove it to your Aunt Ruth's in Cleveland, Ohio, no doubt the cake would arrive somewhat damaged by the trip.

In this analogy, the cake represents an analog telephone signal, which is subject to static interference (the trip). The resulting damage is a loss of signal strength over long distances.

In a digital world, you would bake the cake as before, but you would also document an exact recipe for the cake. Then, rather than driving the cake itself to Cleveland, you would take along only the recipe. Even if you spilled coffee on the recipe; even if you sat on it the whole time; even if you used it to wipe rain off your side view mirrors, you could still bake a perfect copy of your cake when you got to Cleveland.

Can you see the difference? Digital signaling is the recipe that permits you to perfectly reconstruct the original signal, resulting in clear, static-free lines regardless of how far the signal must travel.

Bulk local phone lines and cheap long distance

In addition to cleaner voice transmissions, T1 lines can save you some money when your local telephone company provides the line. Remember, these lines can accommodate up to 24 phone connections. So, due to the economies of scale, your local carrier can usually make price concessions for you, such as a per-line savings for renting the whole pipe. Leasing a T1 line from your long-distance carrier can have an even greater effect on the cost of your long-distance service. Here's why.

When a long-distance carrier places a call for you using your local CO lines as the point of origination, it is called a switched call. Your carrier recognizes three elements of cost for this type of call. First is the cost of moving it along the carrier's network, which may consist of wholly owned, leased, or subleased telephone lines. Then, for the privilege of originating and terminating telephone calls, your long-distance carrier pays the local phone company on each end of the circuit a per-minute fee.

For example, I was a US West customer here in Phoenix, and McLeodUSA was my long-distance carrier. My mother lives north of Seattle, where GTE is the local phone company. When I wanted to call Mom, McLeodUSA would have to pay US West about 1.5 to 3 cents per minute to carry my call to its switch in downtown Phoenix. Then McLeodUSA would have to pay GTE a similar amount in order to terminate my call at its Seattle-based switch over GTE's line to my mother's house.

All together, McLeodUSA's fees to local phone companies for carrying my call would total about six or seven cents. McLeodUSA's accounting department then passes these charges on to me—marked up, of course, to secure a decent profit.

Now, if a long distance-carrier installs a T1 line to your business, a direct connection is created that bypasses the local phone company. Calls that travel via a T1 directly to the carrier are known as dedicated calls. Again, up to 24 calls can come across a single T1 connection at any given time, but rather than paying for each individual line, you are charged a flat monthly fee for the entire circuit. Because this line bypasses the local phone company's switch, though, it can only be used for long-distance calls. The good news is that by eliminating the origination fee—one third of the cost of every call—this type of T1 line significantly reduces your charges for long-distance service.

ANI / DNIS

The digital commands necessary for reproducing a telephone call over a T1 line occupy only a small portion of the bandwidth available for each channel. In fact, only 9 to 16 kbps (kilobits per second) of digital data is needed to produce telephone-quality voice, but 56 to 64 kbps of bandwidth is available on each T1 channel. (For your information, the method of embedding information within the telephone signal itself is called in-band signaling.) Therefore, long-distance telephone companies can use the extra capacity of a T1 line to offer you more services than simply telephone connections.

For instance, on inbound calls to your toll-free number, your carrier can transmit your caller's number together with the telephone signal. This service is called automatic number identification (ANI) and is, in essence, caller ID on a long-distance T1 line. If your phone system is intelligent enough to interpret ANI signaling, it can capture the caller's number to display on your phones and store it for reporting.

Dialed number identification service (DNIS), permits your carrier to provide you with multiple toll-free numbers on a single T1. For example, you could order ten numbers and publish them for different products in a marketing campaign or assign them internally to different departments in your business. You might publish one number as your customer service toll-free number and another number as your main business toll-free number. In this way, you gain the capacity to track your callers by whatever categories you choose.

To track callers without the help of DNIS, all calls would have to come in on separate lines—for example, 800-555-1234 would ring on lines one through five and 888-555-6789 would ring on lines six through ten. In contrast, DNIS utilizes a signal embedded within the call that repeats the last four digits (usually) of the number dialed. Regardless of the T1 channel that the call comes in on, your phone system will recognize which 800 number was dialed.

Phone systems that take advantage of DNIS can interpret the information they receive to route calls to various extensions or departments based on the number that was called. Or you may want your telephone to display which toll-free number is ringing in order to answer it differently from the others.

If it served your purposes, you could have dozens, or even hundreds, of toll-free numbers on one T1 line. By using DNIS and a T1 line, a national answering service could sort its clients' calls, and a customer service center responsible for multiple products could answer different lines with the appropriate script for each product.

ISDN

Profit is important to any business, of course. It's the reason for being in business, isn't it? To make money? Well, telephone companies certainly see it that way. So, as soon as the telcos became aware that the human voice was not the only kind of traffic being shuffled down their lines, they wanted to react quickly with products and services that could accommodate other types of traffic. But, having already invested heavily in their existing network, it was essential that any new technology utilize those same copper telephone lines. One answer was ISDN (integrated services digital network), a digital telephone line.

Digital signaling is the foundation of ISDN service, and it takes the notion of sending information down a telephone wire to a new level. Basically, ISDN works by first splitting a single line into multiple channels. Then, it isolates all the control and signaling information for each channel onto a single channel, the delta channel. In this way, the remaining "bearer" channels are free to carry only content, such as conversations or data.

There are two varieties of ISDN currently available. Let's take a quick look at each.

Basic rate interface

BRI (basic rate interface) is your home variety of ISDN. It consists of a single copper telephone circuit divided into three channels—one channel for signaling plus two bearer channels.

As I mentioned in the paragraph above, the delta channel carries all the digitized signaling and overhead information, and the bearer channels carry the calls.

Using an ISDN modem or telephone with your BRI line gives you the ability to make two phone calls at the same time. In addition, each bearer channel has a guaranteed data transmission rate of 64 kbps, which means your Internet call or laptop dial-up to the office network will have more pep than a regular modem call.

Now, here's where ISDN can get interesting. At each end of the call (at the central office and your ISDN modem), intelligent devices are controlling the bearer channels outside of the signal itself. Thus, if needed, the bearer channels can be joined together to create a single, fat 124 kbps channel for data transmission. The greatest strength of ISDN is its capacity to give you this kind of bandwidth.

Primary rate interface

The big brother of BRI is known as PRI (primary rate interface). It uses a T1 line as its telephone connection, which translates into a lot more available bandwidth. Because a T1 line can accommodate up to 24 channels (remember?), your T1-enabled PRI connection will give you one delta channel and 23 bearer channels of 64 kbps each to allocate as you like. You could bond all those channels together for a really fat data pipe, or maybe you'd prefer 23 quality voice calls.

ISDN in its PRI guise is usually sold as an advanced T1 line, meaning you get more features and capabilities than a regular T1. For example, you can get local caller ID on an ISDN PRI, which will give you a name along with the phone number. Also, if you have videoconferencing equipment, you can get the extra bandwidth you need by grouping channels together and dedicating them for data transmission. When your videoconference is finished, you simply disband the channels to open up your voice connections.

Even though ISDN PRI is sold as a premium service, it does not always cost more than a T1. In some markets, I have seen ISDN priced below standard T1 lines for local service; in others, significantly above. Naturally, it all depends on what the market will bear, who the local carriers are, and the dynamics of competition in your area. Once a carrier is equipped to provide ISDN PRI (because not all are), it is inexpensive to deliver. However, it can be complicated to set up and install, so the decision to purchase PRI should be based on the merits of the technology itself.

In comparison, BRI is sold as either a flat-rate monthly service or a metered service. For metered service, you pay a per-minute or per-hour usage charge plus a monthly connection fee. If BRI service is sold both ways in your area, your choice will depend on how much time you plan to spend on ISDN calls.

DIRECT INWARD DIAL

We all know people who have a private telephone number at their workplace. Maybe it's a friend who works at IBM, or maybe it's a salesperson you deal with who can be reached directly without going through the company's receptionist. Supplying every person in your office with a private telephone line can get quite expensive, however. If your phone company charges $50 per month for a line and your company employs 50 people—that's $2,500 every month!

Personally, I think that kind of money would be better spent on a company game room, or at the very least, free caffeine for employees, but the advantage of private numbers is that your customers can call your employees directly. Though services such as voice mail, call forwarding, and so on certainly have their place in business, enabling your customers to call you directly is a great way to establish relationships. And, as we know, building good customer relationships is essential for maintaining that all-important edge over your competitors.

So, do we just suck in our bellies and pay the money? Not so fast. I want to tell you about a service known as direct inward dial, or DID. Regardless of the type of telephone connection you use—analog circuit or T1 channel—DID can give you a private telephone number for each and all extensions within your business at a reasonable cost.

If you opt for direct inward dial service, a certain number of circuits, or lines, are pooled in your building. Then, a telephone number is assigned to every phone set you choose and those numbers are stacked through the pooled lines. (You can get an almost unlimited number of private phone numbers.) But, you say, if there are only a few circuits serving so many numbers, won't the lines get jammed up? No, because not every number is receiving a call at exactly the same time.

OK, now, pop quiz. Who remembers DNIS? (Yes, you in the back with your hand up.) Isn't that when the long-distance phone company identifies the toll-free number your customer dialed by sending your phone system a few extra digits after the call rings in? Yes, that's right, and direct inward dial is exactly the same technology applied to local telephone service.

For instance, pretend for a moment that a caller dials one of your DID numbers, say the number assigned to Gregory, who is the manager of your customer service department. On "seeing" a telephone call bound for one of your numbers, the central office attempts to grab one of the DID trunks that serve your business. Let's say you have four lines; two are in use, but the third is free. So, the central office picks up that line and signals your phone system (with a ring) to let it know there's a call to deliver. Then, immediately following the first ring, the CO pulses the last four digits of Gregory's number. Your phone system recognizes the four pulses (digits), knows the call is for Gregory, and rings Gregory's phone. That's all there is to it.

Here's a good illustration of DID in action from my personal experience. At one time I worked for a telephone system vendor in Seattle. The company employed 17 or so employees, and we all had private numbers stacked behind four DID lines. I never received a single complaint that a customer could not get through on my private line, and, as far as I know, neither did anyone else. In this case, just four lines provided consistent, open service for about 20 private telephone numbers.

Your local phone company charges a monthly fee for the DID lines, just like regular phone service, plus a nominal fee for each number. It's easy to see that DID can be a cost-effective productivity and communications tool for your business.

OTHER LINES

Thus far we have discussed the basic types of telephone lines and services that you are most likely to use or run into. However, there are one or two others I really think you should know about. So, without further ado, let's see what else those telco engineers have dreamed up for moving a telephone call between their networks and their customers.

Foreign exchange (FX) lines

I currently live in a suburb of Phoenix, Arizona, along with a huge chunk of my state's population, while another sizeable chunk, numbering a million or so people, lives in and around Tucson. Though these two cities are only a two-hour drive apart, they are not particularly good neighbors. The populations simply don't seem to like each other. Could it be the intense football and basketball rivalries between the University of Arizona (Tucson) and Arizona State University (Tempe/Phoenix area)? And what does this have to do with a foreign exchange line?

I'll continue my story. It seems that companies from big, old Phoenix are always attempting to penetrate the Tucson market, but customers in Tucson don't always warm up to an outsider. Tucson folks prefer to keep business in Tucson hands, if possible. Maybe you have a similar business dynamic between two communities in your area. Anyway, doing business in Tucson as a Phoenix-based business can carry something of a stigma. I've even heard it called poaching. It's as though big brother is coming into little brother's room and taking CDs without permission.

Now, a Phoenix telephone number is obviously a red flag to a Tucson native, signaling loud and clear that this business is a poacher. Likewise, a toll-free number (800, 888, 877, 866, and so on) is a dead giveaway that the business may be from out of town. But, if a Phoenix-based business is intent on moving into the Tucson market, there is an option available. Installing a Tucson foreign exchange (FX) line may just muddy the waters long enough to get a chance to do business.

Basically, an FX line is a local number assigned by a local phone company, which, in this case, would then be routed to Phoenix. Ordinarily, telephone calls between Tucson and Phoenix incur long-distance charges, but there would be no charge to Tucson customers calling on an FX line. As far as they are concerned, they have made a local call.

It works in reverse, too. Calls made from the Phoenix office to Tucson across an FX line are also treated as local calls. Even though the phone company doesn't charge long-distance rates on these calls, be aware that it does charge a premium for the foreign exchange service. Some companies may find, however, that an FX line more than pays for itself in increased business.

Ear and mouth (E&M) lines

An E&M circuit is an analog telephone line composed of two pairs of telephone lines instead of just one. Most commonly, it is used as the bearer line for analog DID service and the tie lines you'll be reading about in a minute. (By the way, are you getting comfortable now with all these acronyms?)

Tie lines

As children, we all tried to "telephone" our neighborhood pals by running a length of string between two tin cans across our backyards. But did you know that what we were attempting to create is called a tie line? In essence, a tie line is a direct telephone connection between two points.

We have long since replaced our strings with the phone company's copper lines, but the need for a tie line comes up frequently in business. For example, when conversations, either voice or data, occur almost continuously between the same two offices, it would make sense to run a dedicated telephone line between them. Doing so would enable conversations to take place at any hour or even nonstop 24 hours a day.

Two computer systems could be chattering away in the background without interruption, or two phone systems could be linked in such a way as to act as one. In this case, a person in one office could dial through to the second office as easily as one phone extension dials another.

Tie lines, also called dedicated lines, can be leased from your telephone carrier. For voice traffic, tie lines are single-channel lines that you can lease either alone or in bundles. When the need is for data, we usually see two configurations—either a single 56K line (56 kilobits per second) or a point-to-point T1 line (1.54 megabits per second).

OPX

Another type of tie line is known as an off-premise extension, or OPX. The primary difference between this single-voice tie line and the regular variety is that it is not carried as an E&M signal. Therefore, it is not a live, open circuit 24 hours per day. However, an OPX line is well-suited for businesses that require constant communication among several locations or buildings.

For example, Southern Aluminum Framing in Chandler, Arizona, has a warehouse located a few miles down the street from its offices. Because supervisors need to call the warehouse frequently each day to check inventory status of various products, the company had Qwest (formerly US West) install an OPX line. This line connects to the main office's phone system, thus turning the warehouse phone into an extension that can be dialed only from the office.

At the very beginning of this chapter, I stated that telephone connections are the lifelines of commerce. In this chapter, it was my goal to identify the physical connections of your telephone service and help you understand how they work. The assortment of lines and services I have introduced to you thus far is certainly not exhaustive, but I do believe that I have met my objective. All that remains now is a quick peek into the future.

DATA TRANSMISSION LINES

Data has taken over our world. Sometimes I think I'll just bust if I hear "www" or "dot.com" one more time. Or not. The truth is, the data world has become such a reality that most of us are numbly comfortable with it. And isn't it our own demands that keep the network engineers busy thinking of new and better ways to move data all around the world?

Have you heard of frame relay? Digital subscriber line? Asynchronous transfer mode? These specialized telephone lines belong to a new breed of circuits that largely exist to carry data traffic. It almost doesn't make sense to call them telephone lines. The demand for special types of telephone lines by large companies and call centers has prompted all kinds of new developments. In particular, a technology known as packet switching has revolutionized the way information travels along telephone lines. Let me try to explain how it works.

Let's pretend you have just bought a beach house in Malibu. (I'd like that.) Naturally, you want to move the contents of your bedroom to your new house. So, first you take the bed apart, empty the drawers, take down the pictures—in short, break the room down. Then you pack everything up in boxes and label each box with what's inside. As you load the boxes into your car, you quickly realize that they won't all fit.

Happily, your good friend is also going to Malibu and says he will help you out, but he is detouring on the way to visit his mother in San Diego. Nevertheless, you load up his car with the rest of your boxes and head out on different routes, agreeing to meet in Malibu. It doesn't matter to you how your boxes travel as long as they all arrive at the same destination. Then, when it's time to set up your bedroom, the labels on each box will tell you exactly where everything is.

Packet switching moves data in much the same way. First, however, the information you want to transmit must be converted from its original form to data. Sound waves, for example, must be changed from their original analog form to a representative series of ones and zeros. Then, all the ones and zeros are grouped together in "packets," which will carry them across special data lines. Each packet is labeled with what's inside, where it came from, and where it's going. At the receiving end, the computer knows how to reassemble the contents of each packet and convert the information back to its original form so you and I can understand it.

Because data can be copied and stored easily, networks use ultra-fast methods for moving this kind of traffic. In addition, many data files are compressed to help speed transmission. As data files travel across an open circuit, particularly at high transmission rates, it is quite conceivable that a few data packets can be lost from time to time. Also, should a data network become congested with lots of traffic, packets may be held up until the path becomes free. Neither of these events is a problem for data files, though. A computer file can be completely reassembled from 90 percent of its original parts, and a delay in delivery is undetectable in the file's final reconstruction.

However, the effect of high-speed transmission methods on voice traffic is completely different. Calls delivered with missing information will have holes in the conversations, and delays are obvious. The delivery of these calls is reminiscent of the clipping we experience on cellular phone calls. Also, the overall quality of telephone calls that have been compressed and decompressed decreases noticeably.

Cisco, Bay Networks, and other equipment manufacturers are working to solve the problem of carrying quality voice along with data on our telephone networks. Soon, though, maybe by the time this book reaches you, the problem will have been solved. In the meantime, the new breed of telephone circuit is best used for high-speed Internet access or for connecting the servers between two offices.

Can you believe it? We have finally finished discussing telephone lines. Next, let's talk about equipment.

Section II

Technology Runs the Show

Chapter

4

Telemarketing
Call Centers

. . . .

IS THERE ANYONE TODAY who has not had the experience of being contacted by a telemarketer? For companies that sell to customers whom they cannot approach directly, telemarketing is a fact of life. These companies use the telephone extensively to sell as many of their products or services as possible. Maybe they are selling from a corporate base in one city to clients all over the country, or maybe the sheer number of their clients necessitates using the telephone to reach them. Whatever the situation may be, it is clear that businesses established to sell only by telephone have much different needs than those companies that use other methods to sell their products.

A good telemarketing center focuses on the relationship it can establish with a client over the telephone. Overhead expenditures are not a priority for many of the backroom telemarketing operations I have seen, nor do they have to be. Telemarketers create their entire business image through their telephone connections.

The first telemarketing office I visited was no larger than twenty feet square with a pile of folding tables pushed up along the walls. Telephone cords hung like dirty spider webs down the back of each table with no regard for organization. It seemed to me that the smell of smoke had seeped into every strip of cloth in the place—clothes, carpet, office partitions—while a cracked, paint-spattered boom box filled the room with vintage heavy metal music.

All the agents worked from a printed list of residential customers, which had been bought from a service that specialized in assembling public information. Two telephones sat in front of each of the ten or so telemarketers. The more skilled reps could dial one phone as they wrapped up a conversation on the other, engaging in nearly continuous conversation all the while.

I met one telemarketer who would dial two numbers at the same time, pitch both if they answered simultaneously, and then hang up on the first one that appeared uninterested. His philosophy was that he would rather dial a hundred numbers each hour, hopefully coming across the customer who was agreeable and instantly understood his message, than dial ten times an hour and attempt to force a perfected pitch on resistant clients.

Yes, these are the same people who call you during dinner with the latest offer from your credit card company or long-distance carrier. I'm sure you know these folks pretty well. They call to ask you to start or renew your newspaper subscription or to buy a case of light bulbs in support of a charity for the blind. Or they call you at work selling office supplies. There's no limit to the services or products they can sell.

Telemarketers may go after sales for their own company, or they may be hired by other companies to perform this part of the business. Done correctly, telemarketing is really quite lucrative. (And if this is your business, you know I'm telling the truth!) The trick is to reach as many people as possible in the shortest amount of time. Put another way, a telemarketer's goal is to speak to qualified prospects for as high a percentage of each hour as possible. This is where technology comes in.

T1 LINES

T1 technology seems to be tailor-made for telemarketers. The top two expenses facing any telemarketing outfit are the cost of labor—those people making calls and generating revenue—and the cost of telecommunications services. Leasing a T1 line can help you reduce both of these expenses.

If your agents have to wait for an open line before they can get to work, their productivity goes down and your labor costs go up. Therefore, it is essential that at least one or more lines is available for every employee. As you'll recall, a single T1 line can give you 24 telephone channels. For many businesses, this number would work nicely, but what if your operation only employs five or ten people?

Bringing in a T1 line can still work for you because most carriers will allow you to use just a portion of the T1 pipe. This service is known as fractional T1, and it gives you the option of using only the channels you need rather than all 24. However, you must use a significant chunk of the line—fractional T1 is not available for a single channel.

When dialing local campaigns, your business naturally uses its leased T1 line as 24 local telephone lines. When your campaign goes national, though, the best option is to have a long-distance T1 installed. This way, you'll have 24 long-distance telephone lines at a lower average per-line cost. Although each call still bears a long-distance toll charge, the overall difference between, say, seven cents per minute and five cents per minute adds up to a 30 percent reduction in this one operating expense.

Because a T1 line is a digital circuit, you cannot simply plug in your telephone and start making calls. In your phone room, you'll need something to plug the T1 into. One option is a piece of equipment called a channel bank.

CHANNEL BANK

Channel banks are usually the size of small, rolling travel suitcases. They transform your T1 line into something your business can use—either individual telephone lines, or 24 jacks to plug your telephones or telephone system into. Your channel bank is invisible to your telemarketing staff, and there are no special procedures for using this equipment. As far as your agents are concerned, they are making calls over normal individual lines provided by the phone company.

Technologically, channel banks are relatively simple pieces of equipment, and manufacturers of these devices abound. A channel bank performs specific functions, and (for an outbound call center) it has one basic configuration—T1 in and 24 telephones out.

Actually, I call them "dumb" machines because I have not seen one that can provide any type of management report. No total calls report, no calls-by-channel report, no utilization reports. When we consider that quality statistical information enables you to get the most out of your telecommunications investment, I know you'll agree that such reports are important. (Are there alternatives? Yes, but we'll talk about them later in this section.)

You can expect to pay between $3,000 and $10,000 for a properly installed, functional channel bank. If you have ten employees, that's just $300 to $1,000 per employee. But you may be able to do even better. Long-distance telephone carriers are aware that there are lots of potential T1 customers who lack the

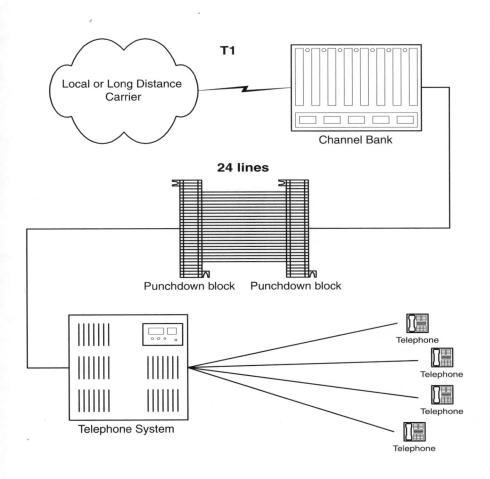

The function of a channel bank
is to break down a digital T1 signal
into individual channels for
delivery to a customer's
equipment.

sophisticated telephone systems necessary to support T1 service. So, many telcos will offer to lease a channel bank to you along with your T1 line for an additional charge of $100 or so per month. Regardless of whether you buy or lease equipment, however, you can be sure that these expenses will be more than offset by the savings you derive from using T1 service.

AUTOMATIC PREVIEW DIALER

The telemarketing center I described in the beginning of this chapter assigned two telephones to each agent. If we multiply two dedicated telephone lines for each rep by ten or so reps, we arrive at a grand total of at least 20 telephone lines being used by this center. Even without long-distance charges, 20 local lines add up to an expensive monthly bill.

However, this company's prospects were almost all out of state, meaning an inexpensive long-distance dialing plan was needed. So, rather than ordering 20 standard lines from the local phone company, this business chose T1 service and got the 24 lines it needed via a channel bank. Good choice.

As the company grew in profitability and experience, its management decided it was time to take the next technological leap. Even though a significant financial investment was required, an automatic preview dialer was selected and installed for the company's call center. This is how it worked.

First, all the company's lists of phone numbers had to be loaded into the dialer's server. Then, as the system dialed the numbers, each phone rep used his computer terminal screen to "preview" the calls. As soon as an agent was finished with one call, another was immediately dialed and previewed by the system.

Most likely, you've had some experience with this technology yourself. Have you ever received a phone call where there was a perceptible moment of silence after you answered, but before the caller came on the line? Yes, that was automatic dialing in action.

AUTOMATIC PREDICTIVE DIALER

Of all the call center devices I have worked with over the years, a predictive dialer is definitely one that can deliver the "wow" factor technology always promises us. They possess a certain magical quality that makes you want to play with them all day rather than do what you're supposed to be doing. At least, I think so—but that's how I behaved when I got my first laptop.

Truly, I can't think of any tool that has created such an overwhelming benefit for the companies that adopt it than the predictive dialer. If your company aims to make a well-scripted, relatively short sales pitch over the phone to the highest number of clients possible, a predictive dialer can revolutionize your business. In fact, these machines are especially designed for outbound telemarketing call centers.

Predictive dialers are actually computers. After taking several mathematical factors into account, these devices will make phone calls to any number of prospects on behalf of your call center's agents. A predictive dialer is usually housed in a PC server that is connected to your T1 telephone lines. It works by running a special software program, which you have previously loaded with your company's client telephone number lists. (Lists are usually imported digitally from a client database of some kind.)

After the number lists are loaded, you next instruct the system on the dialing rules you have decided on—whether "9" needs to be dialed for an outside line; whether the calls are long distance or local; or whether calls must be made in any specific order. Finally, the goals of your campaign are loaded depending on how you want to measure your success rate—mean dials per minute or hour, average conversation length, or whatever you choose.

Individual telephones are then connected to the dialer so that agents can receive the calls placed for them by the system. Some predictive dialers also employ screen pop technology, where client information will appear on an agent's monitor simultaneously with the connected call. Once activated, a predictive dialer grabs its outside lines and screams into action, dialing the numbers on its loaded lists at a furious rate.

Now, how does this machine know whether or not a call is answered by a live prospect? By listening. Really. These computers are programmed to recognize the traditional "hello" of an answered call, as well as the characteristic tones signaling voice mail service or the sounds of an activated answering machine. As soon as the dialer detects an unsuccessful call attempt, it immediately disconnects the line and dials the next number on the list more speedily than any human fingers ever could.

When the dialer does connect with a live person, it transfers the call to an agent in a split second. The agent is alerted that a call is coming in by a short burst of tone, while the client is minimally aware of the transfer. In addition, on systems with local area network capability, the prospect's record simultaneously appears on the agent's computer screen. Can you imagine how precisely timed these machines are? Not only do they maintain the balance between keeping agents busy and not placing calls when agents are unavailable, they go one step further by distributing the good calls evenly among all agents. This is the kind of technology that makes me say, "Wow!"

A onetime customer of mine, Subscription Technicians of Phoenix, Arizona, sold newspaper subscriptions for a variety of publishers to customers all over the country. This company employed about 30 agents and used two predictive dialers to help fulfill the sales goals of its clients. Over time, Subscription Technicians became very knowledgeable about its business.

For instance, this company knew that in any given market an agent must talk to approximately 20 customers in order to make just one sale. It also knew that a high percentage of the telephone numbers provided by its newspaper publisher clients or marketing list companies would result in "no contact." Many times, either an answering machine would intervene or a phone company intercept recording would come on the line, such as "number no longer in service," "number disconnected," and so forth.

Like any company, Subscription Technicians was in business to make a profit for its owners. In order to cover payroll and operating costs, plus the hoped-for profit, the company knew that each agent must close a certain average number of sales per hour. Statistics showed that it took 30 to 60 seconds of conversation with a customer to hear "no," while a five-minute call was generally required to secure a sale.

Prior to installing a predictive dialer, however, agents manually dialing their calls experienced an average of 40 percent no-contact calls. Further, when dialing time, ringing time, and time spent reviewing the call list was added to the no-contacts, it was found that each agent was averaging only 17 minutes talk time per hour. At this rate, agents were unable to get through the statistical 20 "no" calls needed to uncover a single "yes." Imagine how discouraging it must be to realize you need to make a certain number of sales per hour, but you aren't talking long enough to land even one!

By contrast, a well-managed predictive dialer can help your agents average up to 54 minutes talk time per hour—that's a productivity gain of greater than 300 percent. Or, from a labor perspective, we could say that the sales formerly generated by three agents can now be delivered by one. Either way, your business benefits.

It's obvious that the addition of a predictive dialer will change your agents' world. Whether they perceive the change as good or bad will depend on how they are accustomed to working. If they are used to pacing themselves and taking a moment to prepare for each call, the dialer will change things radically.

Now, as soon as they strap on their headsets or sit in front of their phones, the beeps and connections will start. All they'll get is one short tone before it's time to launch into their scripted speech. Then, once that call is completed, there's only a second or two before the next beep comes, and the next, and the next. At the end of an hour, they will have talked to three or four times more callers than they're used to. Some agents may find this tempo too fast, but the aggressive agent who couldn't dial quickly enough will more than welcome all the extra opportunities to make money.

In general, the activity of a predictive dialer is invisible to the public, but sensitive customers can detect this type of call. No doubt you have taken phone calls where you noticed a slight pause before a human voice came on to offer you products ranging from magazine subscriptions to long-distance telephone service. Normally, we are forgiving of technology's impersonal side, but sometimes calls from improperly programmed dialers can be downright annoying.

Have you experienced the call that hangs up on you after a few seconds of silence? In this case, the dialer placed more calls than the available agents could handle. Or what about the call that plays a recorded message asking you to hold for an operator?

Did you ask for an operator? These kinds of calls are intrusive and maddening, but maybe you can take perverse comfort in knowing that it's not only your time being wasted—some business out there is wasting time and money as well.

The purchase of a low-end predictive dialer capable of feeding calls to ten or twenty agents will set your call center back by $10,000 to $20,000. For larger telemarketing centers, the cost could exceed $100,000. Remember, though, that predictive dialers are highly effective tools, which can be customized to increase the overall productivity of your business. As with other call center technologies, a dialer will soon pay for itself when used correctly.

For example, by tripling your agents' talk time, you could see a reduction of one third of your labor costs. If your center pays its agents $2,000 per month, the dialer could save you $4,000 each month in salaries. Or, the same number of agents could each see a threefold increase in contacts per hour, resulting in more sales and thus more profit to put toward the purchase of the system. But that's not all. Once the dialer is paid for, there's no end to how you can improve your call center with all the extra money that becomes available.

I don't want us to leave this chapter thinking that telemarketers are the only people who can benefit from using predictive dialers. Outbound call centers are established for many purposes other than just selling products or services by telephone. Let me offer you a few examples.

Though it's hard to believe, I must admit I am not always a perfect person. More specifically, there have been occasions in my life when the timing of certain billing cycles and the timing of my check-writing days fall somewhat out of synch. Such was the case one hot, spring morning not too long ago. (I should tell you that May through late September is hot here in Phoenix, and the outside temperature this particular morning reminded me of the underside of a poorly maintained Ford Falcon that had just completed a cross-country rally. But you're right—hot weather does not excuse financial forgetfulness.)

When I answered my ringing phone that morning, I heard the familiar pause that told me a predictive dialer was making this call. A friendly financial services agent then came on the line to politely inquire about my overdue cell phone bill, but as we spoke, only one thought ran through my mind: What an excellent application for predictive dialing.

My cell phone provider probably makes a slew of reminder calls to slow payers (such as me) in the first trimester of any month. Later in the billing cycle, another flurry of calls is probably made for true collections. It's easy to see how a predictive dialing platform would give my carrier the most efficient ratio of calls completed to man-hours invested, and the same would hold true for any organization that initiates telephone contact with a large customer base.

Imagine how efficient updating customer mailing addresses would be if you talked only with those customers who answered the phone. And imagine how effective a marketing campaign directed towards every customer in your database would be if the no-contacts were automatically weeded out for you by the system. Consider also how predictive dialers can benefit fundraising efforts when there are potentially thousands of people to call, but only a finite number of volunteers and limited time.

I could go on and on, but let me finish with one last example that illustrates a relatively recent application of this technology. Because predictive dialers are actually computers, they all have the ability to record and store audio. Some call centers now program their dialers to play a prerecorded message whenever a good connection is made. Think of how a political campaign could benefit from 10,000 phone calls dialed the day before an election, each playing a 15-second "get out the vote" message. Best of all, there's no high-cost human labor involved. Depending on the campaign, such intensive voter contact might be worth almost any price.

Keep in mind, however, that a predictive dialer is an expensive technology to own and operate. If you find your pockets aren't deep enough to cover such an expense, you might want to consider contracting with a call center for the use of its services. Known as outsourcers, these centers will hire out their agents and predictive dialers to work on your project. There are scores of competent outsourcers all over the country, and you can read more about what they will do for you in the last section of this book.

Chapter

5

Customer Service Call Centers

DO YOU REMEMBER the last time you called a customer service center? It may have been when you called your local phone company to set up new service for your home. Did you wait in queue? No doubt a recording came on first to instruct you to choose residential or business service. Then, as you were left holding the line, were you politely reminded how much they appreciated your patronage? Did a sympathetic voice frequently come on to tell you how important your call was, and ask you to please stay on the line?

Well, that's how the phone company handles its calls, but what about you? Do you have a general customer service number that anyone can call with questions about accounts or bills? Are these calls taken by the same people that answer your company's sales calls or handle technical issues? Or is there a department or dedicated telephone line within your business that services only existing customers?

Phone companies, airlines, and utility companies are among the many businesses that operate enormous customer service call centers, and you can learn a great deal from them. First, however, let's profile a much smaller business and its customer service efforts.

Matt Wheaton started up a business at home that sold tinting film to body shops and auto supply stores around the country. He put together his own small catalog using Adobe PageMaker on his Mac, and gradually added specialty items to his product line, such as pin-striping, decals, and lettering.

At first, he ran his company out of the spare bedroom in his condo with only one telephone line, a computer, and some postage stamps. Phone orders kept coming in, business grew, and before he knew it, he found himself moving into a three-office suite where he could fill orders as late as 4:30 P.M. before UPS pickup arrived. Soon, his fiancée and younger brother joined him in the daily activities of his company.

Things were clicking along pretty well, and the calls kept coming in. Occasionally, Matt would go out of town to attend trade shows, looking for new products to add to his line. In particular, he looked for obscure items that the stores he supported would be unlikely to stock themselves. When not traveling, Matt worked at his office with his crew, which now included a fourth person dedicated to shipping tasks.

The entire group fell into a comfortable working groove. Together, they were able to manage the frequent spikes in calls by covering for one another, placing calls on hold, and taking responsibility for catching callers off hold.

CALL SEQUENCERS

Obviously, things could get extremely hectic for Matt's business once in a while, such as when five lines lit up and only three people were available to answer; or when Matt was in the middle of a catalog proof and saw that four lines were holding. Some days, the noise was so overwhelming that Matt swore he still heard phones ringing as he lay down at night to recharge for the next day.

As the business continued to grow, spikes in phone calls became more frequent. Matt took a hard look at his books, but he knew he couldn't afford another employee yet. Meanwhile, a competitor had mailed a catalog (strikingly similar to Matt's own) to all the stores and body shops Matt sold to. Plus, some of his customers were beginning to complain about waiting on hold too long when they called.

To top off the whole situation, there were three trade shows coming up in the span of three weeks that Matt needed to attend if he wanted to add the line of chrome accessories he had been thinking about. However, phone orders could not be neglected. There was just no way around it—Matt had to find a way for his limited staff to handle the increasing number of calls.

One easy way out was to employ voice mail service on his business lines, but Matt knew it was important to talk to his customers. Many would simply call a competitor rather than leave a message. Besides, Matt's small, tight-budgeted business specifically needed help only in managing the spikes of incoming calls. After carefully reviewing his options, Matt settled on a call sequencer as the perfect technology to solve his problem.

A call sequencer works by monitoring the telephone lines that come into your business. When it detects that a call is ringing more than a prescribed number of times, it steps in to help out. First, it plays a greeting that lets the caller know all lines are busy, and then it places the caller on hold until an employee has a chance to answer.

The call sequencer is mounted close to where your telephone lines and telephone system interconnect. There, your phone lines are each looped through the sequencer before connecting to your telephone system. Once installed, neither you nor your callers are aware of the device when talking on the line. In fact, call sequencers work very much like our faithful and familiar answering machines. You simply wire them into your telephone lines where they spring to life only when a call is unanswered after a certain number of rings.

Again, we are not talking about a technologically sophisticated device. But how useful would it be to have calls placed on hold automatically during an avalanche of calls? How annoying is it to your work flow, your callers, and everyone else in the room when things must be continuously interrupted to juggle new incoming calls? Have you ever had the following conversation?

"Yes, John, we have that in three colors. Green, gray, and—I'm sorry, I have another call, please hold. Hi, this is Steve, can you hold? Thank you. John? No, I'm sorry, wrong line. John? Yes, now where were we? The third color is—sorry again. Please hold. Hi, this is . . ." What a nightmare!

Call sequencers are modular devices designed to accommodate a predetermined number of lines. You buy the model that fits the size of your business. In Matt's case, he paid just under $3,000 to have a six-line call sequencer installed and set up in his small office. That's far less than the expense of hiring an additional person to handle telephone calls.

When Matt considered how he was surely losing business if his customers couldn't get to him or were inadvertently mistreated, he knew his money was well spent on the call sequencer. Just knowing the technology was there to kick in when needed freed him to channel his energies into growing and improving his business. And that's what call center technology is all about, you know. It only exists to help you be successful. So, let's look at what else is out there.

UNIFORM CALL DISTRIBUTION

Uniform, or universal, call distribution (UCD) is the most common method in use today for parceling out multiple calls to a single number among several telephone lines. If you employ a voice mail system featuring multiple ports, and if calls routed to the voice mail system automatically roll through all the system's extensions until an open line is found, your system utilizes UCD. If you have more than two business lines at your office, and the main number rolls over to an open line whenever the first is busy, you are also receiving the benefit of UCD in the form of "hunting." (I'll describe how hunting works in a minute.)

UCD is generally a function of your telephone system that is set up within the system's programming. It allows you to group together any number of telephone extensions and then assign some basic rules on how calls are delivered to that group.

For example, I once worked for a company that processed credit card transactions over the telephone. There were eight of us working on the swing shift, and I recall that our workload was distributed fairly among us. Our phone system accomplished this equitable delivery by bundling all our individual extensions together in a UCD hunt group. Incoming calls were first delivered to a pilot number, which was a fictitious extension serving as the primary route into our hunt group. After that, we took calls in rotation.

When programming a telephone system for hunting, there are two choices available—terminal or circular. Terminal hunting attempts to connect a call to the first extension number on the hunt group list. If that line is busy, it rolls to each number in sequence until finding an open line. On occasions when all lines are in use, the system rolls back to the first line to start the whole process over again. In contrast, circular hunting first tries the extension immediately following the extension that was last connected. If the fourth extension in the group was the last one to receive a call, the system tries to ring the fifth extension for the next incoming call.

Callers are not aware of all your system's efforts on their behalf. They hear no messages or intercepts, only ringing until an agent comes on the line. However, if a call is unanswered after a certain number of rings, hunt groups often designate an over-flow extension that will bring the caller to a voice mail system or an operator. This strategy prevents calls from getting stuck in an endless loop.

To sum things up, UCD takes care of the balancing act required to present each of your agents with equal opportunities to transact business for you. Compared to other technologies currently available, UCD is not exactly high-tech, but it *is* a good, basic method for call distribution. Moreover, it's cheap. Most phone systems have UCD functionality already built in, and it only takes a couple hours of a technician's time to fire it up.

Reporting

Keep in mind, however, what UCD won't do for your business. It offers no sophisticated call routing, no automatic holding. It won't play recordings for callers to listen to (unless you're willing to install additional programming and equipment), and it rarely provides any type of reporting capability. To my mind, the lack of reporting capability is a serious deficiency.

Large customer service call centers rely heavily on reporting to measure the performance of their workforce, whether individual agents, groups of agents, or the call center as a whole. These centers know that statistical information is virtually the only way to judge the productivity of a group of individuals who handle multiple, short, generic calls. Not only must performance reports be constantly available and totally accurate, they must also translate their compiled information into percentages and averages so it can be compared to the overall goals set for the call center.

For instance, if your call center anticipates 1,000 customer service calls each day, then your staff of ten agents must be able to handle 100 calls each. Is this a reachable goal? Not if your reports tell you that the average talk time between a caller and an agent is three minutes and forty seconds. Ten agents will never cover 1,000 calls in an eight-hour shift.

Agents also need feedback on their performance. Many large call centers base an agent's compensation on how his work performance compares to that of coworkers or how it measures up to preset goals. Typically, you'll see large computer monitors hanging from the call center's ceilings, each displaying a wide array of ever-changing statistics to the agents below. How many callers are in queue? How long has the oldest call been holding?

Keeping track of the numbers helps groups of agents, too. Is the business group outperforming the residential group? Or vice versa? No matter how your agents are organized, they need up-to-the-minute information in order to work most efficiently and meet their goals.

The ability to pull this kind of information out of your system can be critical for your business. In short, it's safe to say that reporting is the key to success for short-call, high-volume call centers. If you agree, you'll definitely want to learn about ACD, the technology we'll discuss in the next chapter.

Applications

· ·

THE FOLLOWING TWO REAL-LIFE situations demonstrate how call center technologies can make a big difference in the day-to-day operations of a small business. In the technology recap sections, you'll note that both businesses also employed a technology we haven't talked about yet—automatic call distribution, or ACD, which is covered in Chapter 6. At this point, however, I thought it was important to give you some examples of the technologies we have discussed so far.

APPLICATION: RESERVATIONS DESK

The Harrymore Hotel had been a condominium building at one time. In fact, the top floors were still occupied by permanent residents when I met its new owner, a lawyer with plans to transform the Harrymore into a five-star boutique hotel.

The building's telephone wiring had first gone into the walls at the same time World War II was making daily headlines. Understandably, after almost 20 years of service, the existing phone system was gasping its last breath. The new owner envisioned a complete overhaul of both the phone system and the related wiring in order to provide the same high level of service his guests enjoyed at other fine hotels in the country.

Like most hotels, the reservations desk at the Harrymore could be reached by a toll-free number. On some days, this number was relatively silent, but most days it rang nonstop, overloading the Harrymore's three reservations agents with calls. It became quite a challenge to keep the reservations line open for potential guests, and although the agents answered every inquiry as quickly and professionally as possible, sometimes it was impossible for callers to get through.

The Harrymore's new owner couldn't afford to staff a reservations desk 24 hours a day, but he didn't want these phones to go unanswered either. He knew potential guests would simply call his competitors if they couldn't reach his hotel. Nor did he want reservations calls going to the front desk during busy hours because the priority for the front desk personnel was to ensure a five-star experience for current guests.

However, it was clear that his reservations agents were in trouble. Their attempts to handle all the incoming calls—by asking callers to hold or juggling back and forth between callers—were only creating a poor impression for the hotel.

Furthermore, there seemed to be a problem with how calls were answered by the three agents. Ideally, the calls should have been distributed equally among them, but that wasn't always the case. If one agent tended to work at a faster pace than the others, that agent ended up with the majority of the calls. It wasn't so much that the other agents were lazy—or were they? It was impossible to measure the productivity of each agent. Conversely, was one agent purposely grabbing all the opportunities to earn sales commissions?

We soon settled on a telephone system that was able to solve the Harrymore's problems concerning both call management and call distribution. Now, when more calls come in than the reservations agents are able to answer, the system plays a short greeting to let a caller know he or she will be attended to shortly.

Callers listen to music while waiting for a free agent, and frequent reminders thank them for their patience. Because calls are placed on hold automatically, agents talk to only one caller at a time. This change alone cut the frustration and noise level at the reservations desk dramatically, resulting in high-quality service for callers.

At slower times, the system delivers calls to available agents in a rotation based on which agent has taken the last call. In this way, the opportunity to make sales is spread among them equally. Almost as a bonus, the hotel was also able to pull reports on the calls that came into the reservations number. The hotel's management could quickly compare how many opportunities for bookings were received on a given day to how many actual reservations were made. Was one agent better at booking than another? Were they losing opportunities at the door? Now it was possible to get answers to these kinds of questions.

Technology Recap

A PBX telephone system was installed for the Harrymore Hotel that featured:

DID capability

Reservation agents are assigned individual telephone numbers so that regular customers are able to reach any agent directly.

Voice mail system

Clients wishing to speak to a specific reservation agent can leave a recorded message for a callback.

ANI

The PBX system reads incoming phone numbers from its long-distance T1 connection; the information is then delivered to individual agents as they answer the calls.

DNIS

This capability permits the hotel to have more than one toll-free number coming in on its long-distance T1. The phone system then routes calls to various departments within the hotel based on which number was dialed.

Automatic call distribution

Reservations calls coming in on the hotel's toll-free number are routed to an ACD queue. Agents log in on the ACD system when they arrive for work in the morning, and calls are distributed evenly among them during the work day.

If all agents are busy when a call arrives, a recorded announcement asks callers to hold; as soon as an agent becomes free, the caller is connected. At times when the reservations desk is not staffed (such as nighttime, Sundays, and holidays), calls are routed to the front desk personnel.

ACD reporting package and call accounting system

These packages collect data on all incoming calls to both the main hotel and reservations numbers. Hotel management can then pull statistical reports for a variety of purposes, such as measuring the productivity of agents.

APPLICATION: APPOINTMENT SETTER

Catherine Cromwell is a lovely English lady who emigrated to this country 30 years ago. When I met her, she worked for a group of three doctors in Everett, Washington. Although everyone in this office answered the phones, only Catherine managed the doctors' schedules. So, when patients called to request an appointment, they were either transferred to Catherine or put on hold if she was already busy.

Frequently, there were times when the number of patients waiting to make an appointment were more than Catherine could handle. In turn, these callers would become frustrated as Catherine's coworkers picked up the line to ask whether they were still holding, and then proceeded to put them on hold again! Understandably, some patients would give up.

Catherine was known for the high standards she set for herself at work, but when rushes like this occurred, so much had to be done in such a short time that Catherine was liable to make mistakes in her haste to get to the next caller. This fact distressed her greatly.

Imagine her chagrin when a patient arrived for an appointment that she had failed to record. Sometimes, the schedule was so tight that Catherine had no choice but to make a later appointment for the patient, and needless to say, both she and the patient were unhappy about that. Though these spikes in calls were not a constant problem, Catherine still felt that she needed help.

For starters, the doctors hired a part-time assistant for her, but, even so, a rush would come and then everything would fall apart. It became apparent that the challenge here was to queue callers. To this end, the doctors decided to utilize a feature of their phone system, which would place Catherine's calls on hold when it detected her phone was in use. Now, she could attend to one caller at a time without being interrupted.

In addition, nurses and other office employees were instructed to transfer callers requesting an appointment to an internal extension number. If Catherine's line was busy, the phone system program would again kick in to play a recording stating that she would be with the caller as soon as possible. Sometimes, of course, patients might not want to hold, so they were also given the option of leaving a message in Catherine's voice mailbox. When Catherine was free, she would call them back to schedule an appointment.

Even though the phone system the doctors employed was much less sophisticated than the one the Harrymore installed—no reporting, no reminder recordings, no queuing to multiple phones—it was sufficient to solve the office's appointment-setting problem. Perhaps most importantly, it significantly eased the life of one dedicated employee, Catherine Cromwell.

Technology Recap

A small, key system was installed with the following capabilities:

ACD

When a caller needs to make an appointment with one of the doctors in the group, the call is transferred to an ACD pilot number. If the appointment agent is busy, the system plays a recorded announcement asking the caller to hold. The system then plays music until the appointment setter is free.

Voice mail system

Callers who do not want to hold in queue have the option of leaving a personal message in a voice mailbox.

Chapter

6

Automatic Call Distribution

. . . .

AUTOMATIC CALL DISTRIBUTION (ACD) systems and software have revolutionized the way businesses offer their services to customers. ACD can transform your everyday business telephone into the consummate tool for improving your ability to offer high-quality customer service.

Every time your customers experience a positive, helpful interaction with your business, the relationship between you is strengthened. And, as we all know, strong customer relationships are the bottom line affecting the very existence and continued profitability of your enterprise.

In the call center world, ACD has had a history somewhat similar to word processors. Let me explain. Remember when computers were new? Lots of people liked to use the early computers as souped-up typewriters, and doing so became known as word processing. Personally, I liked that name. No longer was I writing or typing words—I was processing them, and somehow that made the whole activity far more glamorous. It was fun to think of feeding the words from my brain through the keyboard and up onto the computer screen, where they could be juggled and manipulated any way I liked. (Even if you don't share this fascination, please read on.)

The first word processors had names like Wordstar and Word Perfect. Each program offered a variety of customized features, and you made your purchase depending on which features you wanted to have. As computers became more powerful, the combined intelligence of thousands of programmers working thousands of hours resulted in word processing programs of galactic size and capability. These beasts provided literally hundreds of new ways to manipulate text. But the truth is, only a handful of these features are actually needed.

Today, almost all word processors perform the basic tasks you require. After 20 years of development, word processing programs are quite mature. We take them for granted because, with the exception of a few cosmetic differences and possibly a strong new feature or two, they are entirely interchangeable with one another.

Like the word processor, automatic call distribution (as a call center technology) has been on the market for more than 20 years. It most often appears as a software function on your telephone system, but it can also be purchased as a complete, stand-alone system. Regardless of how ACD is installed, I consider it the best and most effective use of computer intelligence applied to telephone traffic today.

Basic programming differences between one manufacturer's system and others on the market was a problem in the early years. Often, companies interested in adopting ACD were forced to choose a system solely on the basis of whether it would work with their existing phone systems. As time went on, however, such proprietary technologies evolved into a generic core set of features that can be applied across numerous platforms. Though these features may have different names or varying capabilities and limitations from one manufacturer to the next, the base system does the same job across the board.

The first ACD systems were developed with large businesses in mind, but now ACD capability is also built into phone systems designed for smaller businesses of twenty employees or less. This happy fact has resulted from a combination of today's digital technology, increasingly powerful processors, the decreasing cost of manufacturing, and the availability of developers.

Your automatic call distribution system has two main tasks to perform. Its first job is to "rack and stack" callers, and hopefully entertain them while they hold for available agents. Its second job involves distributing incoming telephone calls to the available agents in some kind of logical fashion. Do you want every agent to get the same number of calls in a shift? Do you want all agents to spend the same amount of time on the phone? Or do you want to employ a more sophisticated distribution plan, such as routing certain calls to particular agents only?

You can program your system to do both jobs to your exact requirements, though different systems will offer various levels of capability. However, before we get into a more detailed discussion of how to choose the right system for your call center, let's review how ACD accomplishes the tasks you have set for it.

DELIVERY OF CALLS

Imagine for a moment that your ACD system is actually an employee of yours—we'll call him Al C. Davis. When calls come in on your toll-free number, Al's first order of business is to get them into the hands of your agents. Ideally, the calls should be divided equitably among all your agents, so how does Mr. Davis handle that?

Depending on the way your company measures things, he has a number of methods for distributing calls. One method involves using a timer to keep track of each agent's talk time. Al wants to be fair to each of your agents, so when it's time to deliver a call, he checks his clock and chooses the agent who has been off the phone the longest. This delivery method ensures a relatively even distribution of calls among a group of agents as long as they are all free to take the call.

Another method involves counting the total number of minutes each agent has been on the phone during a particular shift. When Al delivers an incoming call this way, he first chooses the agent who has been talking on the phone the least amount of time, regardless of how many individual calls the agent may have taken. Thus, if one agent has spent 100 minutes on three calls while his coworker has taken 98 one-minute calls, Al will figure that the coworker is entitled to call number 99. That's just the way he sees it.

More sophisticated ACD systems use a method of distribution called skills-based routing. The beauty of this method is that callers are immediately put in touch with the agents best suited to handle their calls. Skill levels do not necessarily imply performance capability (although they could). More likely, your call center supervisor will decide what expertise is required for each level, and then assign your agents their skill levels accordingly. For example, agents at skill level one will know all about product A, while those agents at skill level two specialize in your company's credit policies.

For skills-based routing to work, it's obvious that calls need to be sorted for delivery to the correct agents. How is this done? One way is to have all calls answered first by a recording that offers a menu of topics or products. The caller then chooses the menu item that most closely matches his reason for calling.

Another method involves mapping different telephone numbers to different products or services. PCmusician, a company specializing in software for music studios, utilizes this method. Like most software companies, PCmusician staffs a technical support call center. Each of its products is linked to an entirely different technical support number, so callers are sorted by the number they call in on. In this way, they can be connected immediately to an agent who specializes in their particular software product.

Paths and queues

Well, so far, so good. As long as there are available agents to choose from, our friend Al (remember him?) knows what to do. But, what happens when every agent is already busy? Al knows what to do in this instance, too, thank goodness. In fact, his ability to handle this exact situation is the main reason we employ him. He simply puts the call in a queue.

Queues are the most fundamental programs in your ACD system, and each queue is nothing more than a set of rules for your system to follow. For example, when there are no available agents to take an incoming call, your system may route it to a queue where it will be answered after a certain number of rings with a greeting, such as: "All agents are currently helping other customers. Please hold for the next available agent."

Depending on the programming you have chosen, your callers may hear music or perhaps another recording that asks them to remain on hold and thanks them for their patience. Even better, you can program your system to offer your callers the option of requesting a callback or leaving a voice mail message.

I love the systems that are intelligent enough to inform callers of what position they occupy in the queue or to estimate how long the wait will be. "Thanks for continuing to hold. There is one caller ahead of you," or "Your expected wait time is three minutes and thirty seconds." These numbers are not made up.

..ey are derived from actual, real-time monitoring of the various queues programmed into your ACD system.

Each queue is assigned a phone number within the system, as though it is a separate extension. Any calls that are either dialed or transferred to that extension follow the routing of that queue. Most systems are capable of being programmed with many different queues that can run simultaneously. Thus, you could have a sales department queue, a technical support queue, and a receptionist queue, and each would have its own specific rules.

ACD queue programming is relatively simple and linear. For instance, if your ACD system could not deliver a call after five rings, it might place it in a queue with the following program:

- Play opening greeting
- Play hold music for 30 seconds
- Play first reminder message
- Play hold music for 30 seconds
- Begin flashing the queue status lights on agent phones (to let agents know calls are pending)
- Play second reminder message
- Play hold music for 30 seconds
- Play second reminder message
- Double the flashing speed of queue status lights on agent phones (to let agents know calls have been waiting too long)

This process of alternating music and reminders (plus flashing lights!) would be repeated until the system detected an open line. At that time, calls would be pulled from the queue on a first-come, first-serve basis and delivered to an agent.

However, the programming of a queue has time constraints, meaning there must be an ending somewhere. Callers can't loop in a queue forever, can they? One frequently used option is to reroute a call from one queue to another rather than out to an altogether new place. So, that's what we're going to talk about next.

Groups and overflow

Remember the skills-based routing we talked about a few pages back? A similar, but more basic, method for routing calls is to organize your list of agents into various groups for the purpose of efficiency rather than expertise. Theoretically, all agents could respond to all callers, but assigning certain calls to certain groups has the tendency to speed things along. Your agents will be tuned into the caller's needs even before answering the phone, and your customers will benefit from your agents' readiness to answer their specific questions.

Once you have organized your agents into groups, your ACD system will route calls in the manner you have specified. Also, the system is smart enough to send calls only to available agents, which is certainly an efficient plan. Otherwise, it could spend a lot of time randomly ringing all the extensions and lines in your call center hoping to find a human being to answer. Therefore, when your agents report to work on any given shift, their first priority should be to log into the system and announce that they are available to take calls. This way, ACD will know which agents are currently at work.

So far, so good. With the help of your ACD system, you are organizing your call center beautifully. But let's get back to the problem of the caller who has been perpetually looping in the queue he was routed to. How will your organizing efforts help him?

Let's take Microsoft as an example. I don't work for Microsoft, but I'd be willing to bet there's a whole slew of customer service people taking calls pertaining to its Windows product line. More than likely, there's a group of people fielding questions about Windows 95, another group handling calls concerning Windows 98, and possibly a third group specializing in Windows 2000.

Normally, incoming calls to each group would be queued until agents became available. But what if Microsoft decided that no caller should hold more than three minutes in a given queue? This situation could be addressed by rerouting callers to other Windows queues.

For instance, if a caller holding for the Windows 95 group had reached the three-minute time limit, the system might be programmed to check the Windows 98 group for a free agent. Then, if the caller was still holding after five minutes (total), the system might look for an open agent in the Windows 2000 group. The assumption here, of course, is that every agent is knowledgeable about all three Windows products.

By organizing your agents into groups and your callers into queues, you have the ability to create a high-quality experience for both. Though your call center may receive many more calls than your agents can answer, ACD can provide you with a cost-efficient alternative to hiring more employees.

Interflow

Occasionally, however, you may find that your callers are still holding longer than you deem acceptable or necessary. In these cases, you can program your ACD system to route the call to an entirely new destination. Maybe the call should go to a receptionist, where the caller will have the option of leaving a message or a number for a callback. Maybe the call should go to management personnel, such as the shift supervisor or the department head. Sometimes, call centers forward overflow calls to a special answering service that is used only for this situation.

Keep in mind that your ultimate goal is to provide your caller with the best possible telephone experience. By setting limits on a caller's queue holding time and arranging for alternate destinations when necessary, you will have gone a long way towards ensuring customer satisfaction. Your ACD system enables you to accomplish just that.

AGENT FEATURES

Perhaps it goes without saying that the absolute foundation of any call center is its agents. (I guess I said it anyway.) Whether your call center consists of yourself and one other person or a team of hundreds, you should be aware that today's call center technology can help everyone to work more efficiently, productively, and comfortably.

Does your call center resemble Greer Millwork's? This company employs six agents to take sales calls, and each spends his workday in an oversized room that has been divided into six-foot-wide cubicles. Located in front of the cubicles are steel racks that hold catalogs from every door and hardware supplier they do business with. With those catalogs, a telephone, computer access to the company's inventory, and an up-to-date printout of customer account histories, these guys have everything they need to handle incoming calls—all within arm's reach.

No doubt your call center is set up in a similar fashion. On the one hand, it certainly makes sense for your agents to have all their tools immediately accessible. On the other hand, though, this arrangement pretty much confines your agents to their desks. Because they are not free to get up and go looking for information they may need, it must be delivered to them. This is where your ACD system can help out.

Agents usually need to know the status of the queue they are assigned to, such as how many callers are holding, the length of the oldest call in queue, or how many other agents are currently logged in and taking calls. Your system can provide your agents with this information in the form of advisory messages, alerts, or alarms. Depending on the particular manufacturer of your ACD system, this information may be displayed on each agent's telephone, or it may be provided via a program that runs on each agent's PC.

Call center agents often have performance goals to meet during their shifts. If so, it is useful for each agent to know how well he is doing at any point during the shift. Some systems will do a peg count on the telephone and deliver the information to the agent in the form of a rating. For example, I might start my shift at noontime with a goal of 100 calls in the next eight hours. If I take a break at 3:30 P.M. and see that my rating is 57 percent, I'm doing pretty well. (Does that mean I get to take a longer break?)

Naturally, call center supervisors also need to monitor the work performance and schedules of their agents. What time did they log on for their shift? How many calls did they take? What time did they log out? During the shift, of course, occasions will arise when an agent must be temporarily removed from the system's "available" list.

Most ACD systems give your agents the ability to take themselves out of rotation without completely logging out. I have seen this feature called either "unavailable" or "make busy." Though the system statistically "captures" the event for reporting purposes, it isn't confused with end-of-shift logging out.

Your agents might wish for a little more privacy when powdering their noses, but at least they won't be fired for constantly leaving work early.

Many call centers require their agents to categorize each incoming call for shift reports. A customer service center may want to group calls by problem type, or a sales call center will need to sort calls by the source of the leads. Account coding is an ACD feature that enables your agents to dial a numerical code into the system either during or immediately after an active call. The associated codes then show up with each call on the shift's report.

For example, your center may want to track how each caller found out about the company's service or product—a television ad, referral by a friend, an article in X, Y, or Z magazine. By assigning a code to each source, a call center's management can gauge how effective each of its marketing efforts has been for generating calls.

At the end of each phone call, an agent's PC monitor screen must be returned to some neutral state before diving into the next call. Usually, there is also a bit of paperwork to be completed. Maybe the call needs to be entered into a log book, or perhaps a transaction needs to be closed and submitted. If your center is a customer service shop, there could be a trouble ticket to file. Regardless of what the specific task might be, the agent will need a brief wrap-up period.

Once again, your ACD system can be counted on to help out. If your call center determines that an agent needs 30 seconds to wrap up each call, a special timer within the ACD programming can automatically add that amount of time to the end of each call. In this way, agents are temporarily unavailable to take new calls. A display on each agent's telephone or PC lets him see the wrap-up timer counting down, so he knows exactly how much time he has to finish his paperwork. However, if your agents are ready to take calls before the allotted time is up, most ACD systems will give them the option of overriding the wrap-up timer. Simply pressing a special key on their phones puts them back in business again.

From time to time, your agents may run into trouble during a call, such as not being able to answer a question or find a particular product. Although we would all wish it otherwise, the occasional irate customer may demand more satisfaction that your agent is authorized for or capable of giving. In these situations, most ACD systems allow agents to unobtrusively call in a supervisor while still on the call.

As an example, one system I know of has a supervisor help key programmed right into each agent's phone. If an agent selects the key while on a call, the supervisor's line rings and he is automatically brought into a silent monitoring session with the agent and the caller. By pressing an override key, the supervisor may choose to step in and take the call. Otherwise, the caller is unaware that the supervisor is there.

Most business owners will agree that it's in their self-interest to support their employees as much as possible. Call centers are no different. Though it may sound overly dramatic to some of you, I often think of call center agents as the troops who serve on the front lines of the battle for business.

Just stop a minute to think of how many telemarketers you and I have rejected or how many customer service reps we've harassed. It's easy to see that telemarketing isn't the easiest job in the world. But, by utilizing the ACD features that I have outlined in the preceding paragraphs, you can give your agents the very best tools available to succeed in their jobs.

Fortunately, the features we have discussed so far are basic to most ACD systems, and, depending on the system your business installs, you could consider using many others as well. Meanwhile, now that we've seen what kinds of wonderful things we can do for the troops, let's look at what's available for the brass.

SUPERVISORY FEATURES

I am referring to working supervisors in this section. These are the individuals who patrol the front lines, inspect the work of the troops, and help out when needed. In many smaller call centers, supervisors are also agents, meaning they are responsible for taking calls when not tied up with supervisory duties. To effectively monitor your agents' work performance, keep tabs on the queues, and cast a watchful eye on your center's overall activity, your supervisors need the special tools that an ACD system can provide.

There are probably hundreds of features available to help supervisors command their troops, ranging from simple to sophisticated. For example, you could program an alarm to sound on your supervisor's telephone whenever a caller has been holding in queue longer than a preset time limit, say, three minutes. Or you could program his phone with a series of buttons that indicate the status of each agent on the shift—logged in, logged out, on a call, in wrap-up, and so on. These are the types of simple tools that will greatly enhance your supervisor's effectiveness.

More sophisticated ACD systems can funnel important information directly to your supervisor's PC screen, including full graphical displays of the status of agents, groups, queues, and overflows. These displays allow your supervisors to view your call center's activity in great detail, even down to individual calls. They can see the center's call patterns for the last hour or the last day, and they may also have the ability to pull spot reports from the call center's collected history.

Some ACD systems will actually allow supervisors to make staff changes right from their PCs. One call center I know of employed two groups of agents to handle two different queues. However, if too many callers were waiting too long in one queue, the supervisor could log out agents from the slow group and log them into the busy group as needed, all via his PC.

With so many features available to assist both your agents and your supervisors, it can certainly be a challenge to choose the right system for your call center. Often, you'll find it helpful to look at all of them and then try to imagine how the features of each might play out in your world.

Because it's so easy to get swept away by all the nifty technology out there, you'll need to remind yourself to focus on what you really need. For example, is basic information in the form of a paper report generated once a day enough? Or is there a significant benefit in being able to see the whole call center—every agent, every caller, every queue—in continually morphing color on your desktop monitor? Let's examine these questions a little further.

REPORTING

Whether PBX-based or stand-alone, any decent ACD system can collect and report information about the calls it processes. Reports may be as simple as a brief record noting the date, time, and duration of each call. More advanced systems can report all kinds of statistics, such as when agents log in and out or whether callers hang up after holding for a certain length of time. In addition, these systems can monitor the duration of each step of an incoming call's journey through your center— delivery time, hold time, talk time, and more. Of course, all this peg counting done within the system's software is useless unless there is an outlet for it. In call centers, there are two main outlets—wall boards and statistical reports.

I have already talked about PC screen displays and the trigger buttons or alarms that can be installed on both agents' and supervisors' telephones. These devices are great for delivering real-time information, such as the number of calls on hold, longest call status, or agent status. But have you ever seen the wall boards call centers use? These boards hang above the agents' booths and display the call center's continually changing real-time information just like a stock market ticker tape.

If your ACD system supports wall board technology, it can be a wonderful tool for motivating your agents, providing information, or making special announcements. Examples: "Team 1 has answered 40 more calls than Team 2," or "11 callers in queue; 2 agents logged in," or "The salesman of the week is Tom Flaan." Nowadays, this same banner-style presentation of current call center statistics can also be displayed in a window located on your employee's PC desktop. Agents will never need to look up from their desks! (Is that a good thing?)

Besides displaying the information it collects, your ACD system can also compile historical and statistical reports. Without such reports, you would have to staff, manage, and run your call center on the basis of blind feel and gut instinct. I don't know about you, but I like to base the operation of my business on something more tangible than intuition (though you never want to completely ignore what your gut tells you).

For example, do I need to employ more agents in my call center? To help me answer this question, I could pull a report that would tell me what the average caller holding time has been with my current staff of three agents. If I think this average holding time is excessive, then I have my answer. When will I need to add more lines to my ACD system? If I consult a report that reveals how often all the lines coming into my call center are tied up by either an agent or a customer holding in queue, I can make this decision with confidence, too.

The ability of different reporting packages to sort and compile information varies significantly from one manufacturer to another. For that reason, I would caution any business considering the purchase of an ACD system to be thoroughly informed about the reporting capabilities of that system. Some systems can only generate a few basic reports, such as a daily agent-by-agent report or a call list for the last day, week, or month.

It may be that basic information is all you want or need. However, in business, more information is usually better. Have you ever scratched your head in a private moment and said something like, "You know, local magazine ads in Chicago and Seattle are really chewing up a huge chunk of my advertising budget. Do we get more calls from Chicago or Seattle? If I only knew, maybe I could drop one of the ads." Or, "The early shift wants to start one hour later. Is this a good idea? I wish I could measure when the bulk of the calls are made in that shift and tie it to sales for the day." It's easy to see how useful extra information can be.

As robust and well developed as most of today's ACD systems are, you will find wide differences in their ability to provide you with information. Therefore, I can't stress the following advice enough—pay special attention to the reporting capability of any system that you are thinking of buying.

COST JUSTIFICATION

So far, we have discussed in detail how ACD systems can impact your customers, agents, and management personnel. I'm sure you'll agree with me that upgrading your phone system to include ACD can only benefit your business on all fronts. Now it's time to revisit the question of expense.

To justify the expense of an ACD system, call centers use a formula that converts the time and labor they will save on each transaction into a dollar amount. In Chapter 2, I applied this formula to call center technology in general. Let's now apply it to ACD specifically.

We have seen that an ACD system allows your center to handle more calls with fewer agents because the technology intervenes whenever spikes occur in the flow of calls to your business. For example, let's say you are running five radio ads per day, one each hour on the hour from 11 A.M. to 4 P.M. Following the airing of each ad, your center experiences an immediate spike in calls. How do you staff for that?

Without ACD, you'd have to employ enough people to answer the highest number of calls received at any given point during the hour, or risk losing customers. For our example, let's pretend the center receives 20 calls a minute for the first five minutes after the ad airs, but only three calls per minute for the rest of the hour. In this case, you'd have 20 agents handling the five-minute spike just fine, but for the remaining 55 minutes, 17 agents would have nothing to do!

With the help of an ACD system, however, you could cut your staff to three or four agents. When the inevitable spike hits your center (in the first five minutes after your ad runs), ACD would kick in, hold the excess callers, and then efficiently deliver them to your agents as soon as lines open up. In this way, your savings in labor expenses will soon cover the cost of the system and more.

ACD eliminates the need to overstaff your call center, and you don't have to worry about losing calls during peak times either. Though your business may not experience such erratic spikes in call flow as I have just described, still, you know that spikes do occur during normal business days. In fact, for the average business taking calls throughout the day, spikes typically peak around 10 A.M. and 2 P.M. in your callers' time zone. To clarify this statement, let me give you a quick example.

My publisher is located in New England where Eastern Standard Time (EST) is observed. He tells me, however, that many of his larger customers are West Coast businesses on Pacific Standard Time (PST). Sure enough, he often gets a flurry of calls at 1 P.M. and 5 P.M. EST from the West Coast, where it is only 10 A.M. and 2 P.M. respectively. Unfortunately, though it's peak calling time for his customers, it's lunch time or closing time for him! (He manages, of course.)

The price of call center technology is usually stated in terms of dollars per agent. To figure the total cost of a system, you simply multiply the dollar amount per agent by the number of agents you employ. The industry uses this method of pricing because, as we've seen, savings in labor expenses are often the means for paying for your system.

The average cost of a PBX-based ACD system is between $700 and $1500 per call center agent. If each of your employees makes $10 an hour, and if implementing ACD increases the productivity of each by three percent, you will save enough in raw labor costs to pay for the system in one year. Or, if installing an ACD system allows you to cut your staffing by ten percent (for instance, nine agents instead of ten), you can defray the expense of the entire system in just a few months.

We have spent a great deal of time examining the attributes of automatic call distribution systems and technology, and with good reason. Once you install an ACD system in your call center, your business will be dramatically transformed on virtually every level, perhaps in ways you couldn't have imagined. Still, there other call center technologies that you'll want to consider using as well, such as an automated attendant, voice mail, or an interactive voice response system (IVR). In the chapters that follow, we'll explore the benefits of utilizing these important business tools.

Application

DESPITE THE MANY SIMILARITIES that certainly exist among the technologies I have described so far, don't be fooled into thinking they are all basically the same. There are distinct and important differences that you should be aware of. Also, for any technology to achieve the results you are looking for, you must first know exactly how you want things to be handled in your business.

Believe me, there's nothing more frustrating than having invested your hard-won capital into a phone system that presents you with unwanted limitations when you try to upgrade or make changes at a later date. The story below will illustrate my point.

APPLICATION: INBOUND SALES OFFICE

Do you recall reading briefly about my client, Greer Millwork, in Chapter 6? This company is in the business of supplying doors and related peripherals to construction companies and builders. Because the owners of Greer Millwork had a very clear idea of what they wanted from their phone system, together we were able to define precisely how calls should flow into their six-man sales center.

When you walk into Greer Millwork's office, the call center is the first thing you notice. You can't miss it. In fact, I found it to be a dynamic environment. In addition to a telephone and a computer terminal for accessing the inventory system, each salesperson was flanked by racks of catalogs representing more door manufacturers than I thought possible. Though a few accounts were handled exclusively by one or another particular agent, in general, the incoming sales calls were up for grabs.

You'll recognize this situation from other examples I have written about in this book. First, to be fair to its agents, Greer Millwork needed to find a way to distribute calls evenly among them. Secondly, this company was well aware that customers placed on hold in a queue may choose to hang up and call the next supplier on their list. Therefore, Greer also wanted to find a way to effectively handle callers when they outnumbered available agents.

Part of Greer's solution was found in the layout of its office. Because the call center was not physically isolated from other employees, sales calls could be answered by non-call center staff when necessary. So, we settled on a phone system design for the call center that would include a bell installed in the office ceiling.

Whenever a caller had to be queued, the bell would ring to signal other people in the room to pitch in. They would do so by simply selecting a pickup key on their own phones to pull the next caller off the queue. In this way, all callers would receive almost immediate attention, resulting in minimal lost sales and healthy business growth. It sounds like the quintessential American success story, doesn't it?

However, like most of us, Greer Millwork was greatly concerned with preserving precious capital for inventory and other business needs. At the last moment, a competitor of mine knocked on the door, took a look at our design for the call center, and promised a system featuring the same capabilities at a lower price.

I don't fault Greer Millwork for buying a cheaper system. If the capabilities of the two systems were identical, I'd do the same.

Unfortunately, UCD (universal call distribution) is not ACD (automatic call distribution), and they do not perform interchangeably. Only a month or so after installing my competitor's system, Greer Millwork called to have it removed. The next phone call was to me: "Steve, I need that system of yours after all. The one we bought was supposed to do the same things as yours, but it didn't. It does something called UCD. . ."

To make sure the technology you purchase is right for your business, you must first focus on your needs. Next, do a little research and find the technology that will achieve your objectives. After that, I strongly urge you to ignore all other available technologies and concentrate on selecting a manufacturer and an installer. Your choices may be limited in these areas, but keep in mind that you already know which technology you want. Don't be sold into anything else!

Technology Recap

Though individual agents at Greer Millwork were encouraged to develop special relationships with certain customers, all agents were required to answer incoming sales calls. The company's goal was to answer calls as quickly as possible and keep customer holding time to a minimum. With a key/hybrid PBX underlying its phone system, Greer utilized the following capabilities to round out its call center:

Voice mail system
   Customers can avoid waiting in queue by leaving a message for a callback.

Automated attendant

Callers dialing Greer's main telephone number are given the choice of dialing an extension directly, routing themselves to a particular department (such as sales), or holding for an operator.

ACD

When all agents are busy, the ACD program queues incoming calls.

Digital announcers

Three separate announcers play recordings to callers in queue. The first asks callers to hold when all lines are busy. Twenty seconds later, a second recording apologizes for the wait and asks the caller to continue to hold. The third recording alerts the caller that an agent will be on the line momentarily.

Night ringing bell

After waiting through all three recordings (approximately one minute and thirty seconds total), callers are transferred to an extension number that triggers a bell to ring. This ringing bell notifies everyone—accounting staff, receptionist, general manager—that a caller has been holding too long. Anyone at any phone in the immediate area can then answer the ringing bell extension by dialing an access code.

ACD reporting capability

Greer Millwork took advantage of the basic reporting system provided with its phone system. This reporting package is rather limited, but sufficient for the company's purposes. It is able to compile simple, peg-count reports, but data is not saved. Once a report has been run, the data is erased from the system's memory.

Call accounting system

A PC-based call accounting software package allows Greer to monitor call traffic, both inbound and outbound, and review the utilization of its lines. Data is sorted by extension, and extensions can then be grouped into departments for reporting.

Chapter

7

Handling Voice Calls

· ·

EACH AND EVERY CALL that comes in on a company's telephone line represents the potential to do business. Therefore, how these incoming calls are handled is a major concern of any enterprise.

Many companies funnel all incoming calls to a receptionist, who first determines the caller's intention before connecting the call to the appropriate party. Some offices hire several individuals to share the role of receptionist, but in many small offices, a single employee performs receptionist duties in addition to his or her regular job.

The telecom industry was quick to realize that a majority of business callers know exactly who they want to speak to before they dial their calls, whether a specific person or a specific department within your business. That being the case, those same savvy folks asked, "Why not have a machine answer the phone and let callers direct themselves?" And so it was. With a wave of technology's magic wand, automated attendants came among us.

AUTOMATED ATTENDANTS

Well-designed automated attendants can function as much more than simple robotic receptionists. No doubt you've experienced the cheery helpfulness of an automated attendant yourself. When telephoning many businesses, the first voice you'll hear is that of a recorded message. Normally, you are thanked for calling ABC Conglomerate, and then you are instructed to dial the extension number of the person you're trying to reach.

If you don't happen know the extension number you need, a menu will direct you to press certain keys for certain destinations, such as "1" for the sales department, "2" for the service department, "0" for the operator, and so on. Other menus may branch out from this main menu, but the whole shebang, start to finish, is the work of an automated attendant.

There are three ways you can implement this technology in your business. The easiest way is to check your existing telephone system—it may have automated attendant capability built right in. Just have the software turned on by your vendor, and then add a device to play the up-front greeting or announcement. Depending on your phone system, your callers will have single-digit dialing access to nine departments or individuals (plus "0" for the operator), as well as the ability to dial by extension number. Some systems provide both extension and single-digit programming for individuals or departments.

An add-on voice mail system is a second method for acquiring an automated attendant for your business. In this case, your announcement or greeting is treated as a mailbox in the system. All incoming calls are first routed to this voice mailbox, and after the message plays, callers have the option of either dialing an extension or choosing from a menu.

If your phone system lacks both automated attendant capability and voice mail, don't despair. Some manufacturers also offer stand-alone versions. These devices are wired directly into your telephone lines ahead of your regular phone system. When a line rings, they jump in to give your caller the same dialing choices as a built-in system. Once a choice is made, the auto-mated attendant then transfers the call via the phone system.

Many hotels use stand-alone automated attendants rather than staffing a live operator through the late night and early morn-ing hours. Calls received before and after regular lobby hours are picked up by the automated attendant, so callers can direct themselves to the guest rooms they want to reach.

Naturally, when businesses install automated attendants, the workload of their receptionists is significantly reduced. If 80 per-cent of your callers opt to self-direct their calls, then your em-ployee is freed up to work on other projects. Also, if you have ever hired extra help in the past to answer calls at busy times, imagine the money you will save in this one area alone.

In my experience, the cost of adding automated attendant capa-bility to your company's phone system ranges from a few hun-dred dollars on up to $1,000 or more. Stand-alone automated attendants run anywhere from $700 to $2,500 depending on the number of lines that need to be covered.

Even if automated attendant capability is already a component of your voice mail system, you may still need to part with some cash. Why? Because your existing voice mail may not be able to handle an extra load of incoming calls on top of your usual mes-saging needs. The only solution is to purchase a larger system.

Regardless of the money you spend to add an automated atten-dant, you'll find the cost is only a fraction of what you'd pay a full-time receptionist. And the upside can be huge. Front-ending your call center with an automated attendant allows your callers to choose their fate—transfer to a specific extension, hold in a queue, or speak with the operator. In fact, I believe that giving your customers the freedom to self-direct strongly reflects the respect your business has for them. Time is a valuable commodity for us all, and enabling your callers to quickly reach the party they want certainly saves them time.

Have you ever had the experience of calling a business where you had to repeat your name and reason for calling over and over and over again? Though all you want is to quickly check a price with your sales rep, Joe, you can't get to him until you speak to the PBX operator, who transfers you to the receptionist in sales, who then transfers you to the sales department's secretary, who finally gets Joe for you. Perhaps I have exaggerated this process a bit, but an automated attendant can totally eliminate the aggravation of wading through any such chain of command.

Now I know that some people are quite opposed to having their telephone calls answered by a machine rather than a human being. But, despite our personal likes and dislikes, it is a fact that automated answering is universally accepted in business today. Indeed, the business world seems to embrace each new breakthrough in telecommunications almost as soon as it is introduced.

Cellular phones, Palm Pilots, and laptop computers are only a few examples of the high-tech devices considered standard by most business people nowadays. Compared to these modes of communication, an automated attendant is almost old-fashioned. However, for those callers who insist on speaking only to a live person, there is always the option of dialing "0" to reach an operator.

VOICE MESSAGING SYSTEMS

Ah, voice mail. Depending on your perspective, it is surely the most wonderful or the most hated development in business messaging today. Let me tell you how it all began.

Back in the early to mid-1980s, Active Voice was a tiny company consisting of three individuals. They were already involved with developing the technology that would allow basic voice mail, but their genius was to consciously adapt it to an innovation that they believed would revolutionize business. How right they were. The cutting-edge technology they were tying their efforts to was none other than our beloved PC—the personal computer.

Answering machines at that time used cassette tapes to make recordings of voice messages left over the telephone. Then, a computer lab located at the Massachusetts Institute of Technology found a way for devices to "listen" to an audio signal (such as the human voice) and convert it into a digital file consisting of the ones and zeros that computers love.

As a result of this development, computers could manipulate digitized voice recordings just like any other digital file. Phone messages could be easily copied, stored, sorted, and compiled into databases, all of which are the basic functions of voice mail. In truth, a voice mail system is little more than a managed database packaged into a software program that enables users to access the information.

The new voice mail technology was viewed as a natural expansion of the telephone system, and it was rapidly adopted by many of the larger telephone equipment manufacturers. Such companies as AT&T, Northern Telecom, and Rolm either manufactured or commissioned huge, specially designed computers to add voice mail capability to their PBX phone systems. Because these first systems were considered quite reliable, the use of voice mail spread quickly throughout the business sector.

Early manufacturers liked to brag about the reliability of their voice mail systems. Even though voice mail is essentially an ordinary computer running a software application, these out-fits insisted that reliability like theirs could be experienced only by using manufacturer-supplied hardware with the systems they sold. Fortunately for us, software companies knew better. In response to this situation, Active Voice, the three-man company I mentioned earlier, decided to buy IBM PCs and clones right off the shelf of the local computer store and build voice mail systems from them.

The big manufacturers countered that they could make a better voice mail computer if they made it themselves. They said the PC was unreliable, and they were right at first. But, as we all know, the personal computer evolved at an amazing pace, rapidly acquiring levels of processing speed and computing power that no one could have predicted. And, even as the capacity of a standard PC soared, its cost dropped to unbelievably affordable prices. In no time at all, the big, proprietary manufacturers found themselves sitting on outdated, overpriced technology.

In addition, PC-based manufacturers of voice mail systems also had the advantage of being able to focus strictly on the program itself. By perfecting their voice mail software and supplying inexpensive hardware, these companies took over the voice mail market in virtually all areas but the very largest enterprises. To be fair, however, I should tell you that most of the proprietary manufacturers long ago adopted the standard PC hardware as their own. Today, it would be extremely rare for a vendor to propose a voice mail system that is not built on a standard PC.

Voice mail has grown into a mature, standard application in the past ten years, and whether you love it or hate it, you can be sure it's here to stay. So, in the next few pages, I'm going to give you an overview of the options available to you. The speedy development of voice mail technology has resulted in the use of two types of messaging servers today—the voice mail system and a unified messaging server. Let's look at the voice mail system first.

Voice mail

Most standard voice mail systems perform three specific functions for your business. First of all, your voice mail system will stand in as an answering machine for you and every employee in your business. Although voice mail messages are routed to individual mailboxes, be aware that a voice mailbox can be shared. For example, your human resources department may have a mailbox that anyone in the department can access. Likewise, your sales department may have a mailbox for taking leads, or technical support may have an emergency mailbox, which will automatically page whomever is assigned "on call" duty.

Voice mail systems offer you a host of options that an ordinary answering machine can't, such as forwarding messages to others in your business. You may also have the capability of recording one or more personal greetings for your callers that can be useful for notifying them of your current availability as it changes or directing them to a coworker.

When messages are waiting for you, different systems use a variety of methods to alert you, such as flashing a light on your telephone, paging you, or even calling you at home if it's after work hours. Some systems allow you to speed up your messages as you listen to them, slow them down, or skip past a message without listening to the whole thing. Still others utilize caller ID to let you know when the message was received as well as the phone number of the person who left the message.

On your caller's side, a voice mail cum answering machine provides them with more options than the traditional: "Please leave a message after the tone." Many systems allow your callers to review their messages before leaving them and even tag the message as "urgent" when necessary. Callers may also have the option of dialing "0" to reach an operator if they prefer not to leave a message at all.

Secondly, your voice mail system can double as your receptionist. Many of the features I described above could certainly do the job of an automated attendant for your business.

Lastly, your voice mail system furnishes you with a cost-effective method for providing basic information to your callers, such as directions to your office, show times of your latest production, or the closing date for bids on your latest construction project. Recording this type of general information in listen-only mailboxes is an easy and convenient way to tell your callers what they want to know, and you save the cost of paying an employee to relay the same particulars over and over. Naturally, callers may have other questions as well, so be sure to give them the choice of speaking to a human being, too.

Unified messaging

Many moons ago, the folks at Active Voice predicted to me that one day you and I and everyone we know would be able to communicate with one another in so many different ways that we would hardly know where to turn first. They coined a name for this emerging problem—infoglut. And it's here. Do you use email at work or at home or both? Does your company have a website? Do you ever need access to faxes or voice mail or email when you're traveling?

To combat the problem of infoglut, unified messaging was developed to round up all these disparate messaging technologies and put them under one roof, so to speak. More specifically, unified messaging is banking on the fact that many of us today find ourselves facing a computer screen whenever we need information. So, that is exactly where unified messaging technology will assemble all your info for you—on your PC desktop.

Let me tell you how. First, unified messaging gathers your voice mail and fax messages and puts them into your email inbox. Then, everything is put together so that you can view, sort, forward, and reply right from your desktop.

For example, faxes are still sent to you in the usual way, except that your messaging server now answers the phone and captures pictures of the documents being faxed. You can then view these pictures on your computer screen and decide whether to print, save, or otherwise manipulate them. Voice mail, too, is handled by the same messaging server. To the outside world, however, it appears that a voice-only system is in use.

The manufacturers of unified messaging systems are frequently the same people who supply voice mail systems. This more sophisticated technology has simply allowed them to expand on the products they already offer. The advantage inherent in utilizing unified messaging is that business communications become incredibly efficient. If your business receives a high volume of communications from customers or clients who use a combination of telephone, email, and fax, then unified messaging will assure you an edge over your competitors.

Another advantage of unified messaging is its ability to take over whenever you are out of your office. Have you ever had the experience of tooling about, doing your business, when you suddenly remember that you need to check your messages for the day? In the past, you scurried to the nearest pay phone and dialed your answering machine to retrieve your messages. Or maybe you connected your laptop to one of those business traveler workstations and logged in for your email. Or maybe you zipped back to your hotel to pick up the faxes that your office had been sending all day. To make sure you got all your messages, you would need to check all three places, and that could certainly be inconvenient. I should mention here that there are email systems that can forward messages to a pager on your belt, but you'd still need a way to retrieve your faxes or voice mail.

Unified messaging can take care of everything in one simple phone call. Because telephones are located virtually everywhere, voice mail is always available to you. All you have to do is dial in and listen.

But what if your voice mail could read your email messages to you as well? What if you could actually respond by recording a message that would be transmitted over the Internet as a ".wav" file (a computer sound recording)? Just contact your neighborhood unified messaging vendor, and you can have this kind of technology working for you and your business in no time at all.

Ports

The integration point between your voice and the digital world on any voice mail system is a telephone connection known as a port. All voice mail systems feature a number of ports, each dedicated to a particular task, such as playing or recording messages. Before purchasing a system, you must first determine how many ports your business will need. How many of your employees might be checking messages at the same time? How many callers may be leaving messages at the same time? Or how many calls might the automated attendant answer at the same time? Surprisingly, the total may be less than you think.

In the mid-1990s, Tri-Tec Communications of Kent, Washington, employed 17 or so reps, including me. Our business was to sell, install, and support both phone and voice mail systems, so the entire staff was not only knowledgeable about telephony, but also adept at using all the telecom technology available at the time. In other words, we used our phone system's various features extensively.

Nonetheless, the company's two-port voice mail system was adequate for us all, and though I received an average of 10 to 15 messages per day, rarely did I get a busy signal when attempting to access my voice mail. However, we didn't use the automated attendant function of our system. If we had, that would have easily doubled our port need.

A good rule of thumb for determining how many ports you'll need is one port for every ten users or less. If your business employs an automated attendant, I would recommend a system with a minimum of four ports.

I am winding down my discussion of voice mail now, so I hope you are becoming convinced that it is a vital need for your business. Your callers expect it, your competitors use it, and it can make all the difference when nurturing those special one-to-one relationships between a customer and his particular sales rep.

From my own experience, Greer Millwork is a good example. Though there are six salesmen staffing its call center, I have dealt with a guy named Max most of the time. Max and I have established a relationship, and I prefer talking to him when I have business with Greer because he knows my buying history and he treats me well. However, I know he can't take a direct call when he is responsible for answering calls in queue, so I like to leave him a voice mail message with my order. When business dies down a little, he can take himself off the queue and return my call.

I appreciate being able to deal with Max directly, and although I am only one customer, I bet your business has many customers who feel exactly the same way.

In general, a voice mail system will benefit your call center, but there is one pitfall to guard against. Sometimes, agents and management both may hide behind voice mail to avoid taking calls when they should or could. Obviously, leaving your customers totally in the care of a machine is definitely not a good business practice.

WHAT ABOUT THE PRICE?

So, which kind of voice mail is best for your business—a traditional system or a unified messaging platform? As with so many other choices, money may be the deciding factor.

Usually, voice mail systems are priced on the basis of either the number of available ports or the number of features offered. To bring the cost down, some manufacturers will offer systems with reduced capabilities, such as removing the automated attendant option or limiting user mailboxes to 100 or less.

I have seen small voice-only voice mail systems priced at less than $2,000, while systems supplying anywhere from six to 24 ports will run about $1,000 per port. However, if you figure that each port will support eight to ten users, you may find that the cost of a voice mail system can be justified as easily as any other type of productivity software.

INTERACTIVE VOICE RESPONSE SYSTEMS

Balancing my checkbook used to be a chore that I hadn't quite mastered, and I hate to think of the time and money my ineptness in this area cost me. Nowadays, though, I call my bank's toll-free number once or twice a week and ask its automated system to read me the credits and debits that have posted. Then I check them off in my checkbook's register and, like magic, my balance is up to date.

I love this system. A three-minute phone call is all it takes to get the information I want, and I don't even have to speak to a bank employee. In fact, that's the real beauty of an interactive voice response (IVR) system. This type of call center technology is very attractive to banks and other businesses precisely because it reduces staffing needs.

Though callers always have the option of transferring to a live operator, the majority of questions can be handled by the IVR system, resulting in significant savings in a company's labor expenses. This reason alone has persuaded thousands of businesses all across the country to install IVRs.

Technically, interactive voice response systems are identical to voice mail systems, just tweaked for different functions. IVRs utilize the same types of ports as voice mail, so the computer at the bank (or other business) can recognize both the human voice and the tones pressed on your telephone's keypad. IVRs can also play recordings over the phone connection that prompt the caller to select options from different menus—"1" for your current balance, "2" to check deposits, or "3" for debits and checks.

The primary difference between an IVR server and a voice messaging system is that IVRs are connected to a company database of some kind. In this way, the system can access the caller's account and any other information needed to answer customer inquiries.

Let's use my bank as an example. When I first call into the system, I am answered by a port. Then a greeting is played and

IVR Programming Software (screen shot)

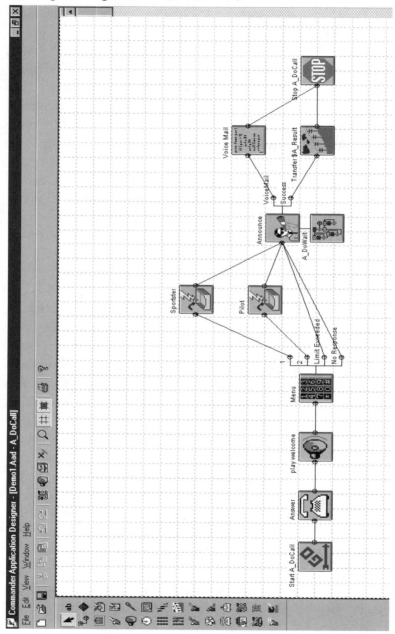

I am told to choose from among various options, such as looking up account information, transferring money, applying for a credit card, or securing help from an agent.

I select the option that will give me account information, and the system then asks me to enter my account number. Once the computer has my account number, the voice server verifies that the number I entered is a valid account. Then I am asked to enter my social security number (to make sure I am me).

After this number is verified, the system reads off my account balance to me and offers me a new menu. If I choose, I can check current postings, deposits, the balance of my overdraft account, or return to the original menu. By simply pressing keys on my Touch-Tone phone, I can request all manner of information about my account. For me, that's wonderful.

As I mentioned above, banks and other companies love IVR because there is minimal human intervention. Previously, if I couldn't wait for my statement to arrive in the mail, I would have to call my bank branch directly to have my questions answered. There, some poor employee would have to pull my account up on his screen and patiently read me the answer to every question. Just think of how much time the bank used to spend with me, and then multiply that by all the other checkbook-challenged folks out there! There are lots of us, you know.

Besides banks, there are hundreds of other businesses that have adopted IVR systems. Have you ever called an airline to check the status of the flight you're going to take later in the day? Have you ever traced a catalog order or a UPS shipment? What about your credit card company? Many employ an IVR so that customers can dial up and find out how close they are to their credit limits or when their last payments were posted.

Let's say your business is an authorized dealer for a certain manufacturer's product. Would it be helpful to your customers if they could reach an automated system after work hours and place orders for the next day directly over the telephone?

Or let's say your business offers a product or service that customers need to check on frequently. Wouldn't it be helpful to have their account information available to them at any time, rather than requiring an employee to answer every call?

American Consumer Debt Services is a company that attempts to serve both debtors and creditors. Its goal is to help consumers mired in debt to avoid bankruptcy. At the same time, it also helps creditors collect on legitimate debts by mediating the payment process between its clients and their creditors.

One of the greatest problems for this business is the sheer volume of telephone calls it receives from both clients and creditors checking the status of accounts. Clients want to know when their payments are received, when their creditors are paid, and when the next payment is due. Creditors want to know many of the same things, plus they need to verify whether clients are actually in the system and making payments. Because all this information is readily available in database form, ACDS estimated that 30 to 50 percent of its incoming calls could be handled by an IVR system.

The net effect of installing this technology would be twofold. First, the call center could handle a greater total volume of calls, and the existing staff could spend more time with callers who really needed to consult an agent. Secondly, the center could get away with hiring fewer new agents even while business continued to grow. In this way, ACDS could easily justify the cost of installing an IVR system strictly on the basis of savings in labor expenses.

Small call centers can take advantage of the basic IVR capability that is built right into some voice mail systems. Both Toshiba and Lucent offer this type of system for a few thousand dollars more than standard voice mail systems. Naturally, there are limits to implementing IVR in this way, including which databases the system can communicate with and how much information can pass through the system to the user.

For dynamic applications such as those used by ACDS or my bank, a custom-tailored IVR program is written to run on a voice server. It takes into account sophisticated call flows and complicated database integration, and the cost will vary greatly. Remember, though, if you add up what it costs to staff a call center with human beings, you'll see that there's a ton of money on the table to pay for an IVR system.

At ACDS, hiring 10 to 20 fewer agents meant a savings of $300,000 to $500,000 in one year. A high-end IVR can certainly cost your business half that amount, but it will work 24 hours a day all year through without breaks, vacations, or medical benefits. IVR allows a business to provide around-the-clock, consistent, high-quality service at a much lower cost than employing human beings.

Another important feature available on most IVR systems is management reporting. Because an IVR system completes all its transactions electronically, it can compile reports for your center's management that reveal who the callers are, what they needed to know, and how long they stayed in the system. Such reporting might be used to charge the cost of a call back to a customer. For example, banks often charge an access fee for dial-by-phone service.

Due to the customized nature and high price tag of IVR systems, they are mostly found in larger call centers. However, in addition to the voice mail systems with limited IVR capabilities described above, smaller call centers should be aware of the lower-priced IVR systems especially tailored for small businesses. Offered as kits, these systems let you program your own IVR with the help of a software tool provided by the manufacturer.

As you begin your search for the IVR system that's best for your business, take a look at the list of publications I have put together in Appendix B at the back of this book. In particular, you'll want to check out *Call Center Magazine* and *Teleconnect*, both of which publish annual roundup reviews of the latest in IVR technology.

Application

HAVE YOU EVER NEEDED TO CALL a technical support line for help with a software program you bought? If so, how would you rate the help you received? Did you get to speak to someone right away, or were you shuffled around from one rep to another? Were you ever asked to leave a phone number for a callback? And most importantly, was anyone able to solve your problem?

For businesses that sell technical or software products, providing technical support via the telephone is a necessity. However, a customer's experience with a support team can vary enormously. The Microsofts of the world may employ hundreds of technical support people whose entire workday is devoted to assisting customers with their questions. Meanwhile, your local Internet provider may have a support staff consisting of two or three reps who have other jobs to do as well.

The sheer number of available agents at a Microsoft-sized business might ensure a quality customer experience, but modern call center technology gives smaller businesses the ability to offer high-quality technical support, too.

Application: Technical Support

PCmusician, based in Redmond, Washington, is a software company that has carved out a special niche in the music industry.

It manufactures programs that permit an electronic musical instrument, such as a keyboard, to interface with a standard PC. By using such programs, musicians are able to simulate a production studio right on their computer screens.

I have found that modern musicians are surprisingly savvy about today's technology because computers have encroached so deeply into their world. However, PCmusician's software is not geared for professional musicians. Its primary targets are students, small-time musical directors (such as for church groups or amateur community theaters), and musical hobbyists, among others. These folks tend to be novices regarding the technology used in the music world, so the help desk at PCmusician tends to receive quite a few calls.

Like other software companies, PCmusician includes technical documentation with each of its products. Although this litera-ture is meant to be as comprehensive as possible, customers are referred to other resources as well. For instance, they can dial in and listen to recorded information concerning common problems; they can log onto the company's website where FAQs (frequently asked questions) are answered; or they can email their questions to the company.

Nonetheless, PCmusician still gets lots of phone calls, so sup-porting its products over the telephone is absolutely necessary. It is also expensive. The agents who staff the help lines obvi-ously need to be proficient users of each product. They must also possess a high-level understanding of computers in gen-eral, not just their own personal computers. And don't they need to be part psychologist as well to handle all the many different personalities calling them on the phone? In short, these employees must be highly skilled in many areas, and that trans-lates (justifiably) into a highly paid employee.

In fact, many software companies find that a tech support department is a costly drain on the inherent profit of its products. So, a tug-of-war ensues in many businesses between maintaining great customer service and minimizing the cost of the help lines. What to do?

In PCmusician's case, its management began by identifying two main problems to address. Problem number one was how to get customers to use all the different help resources that the company offered them. How could customers be encouraged to visit the website, email their questions, dial in to listen to recorded hints and tips, or read the documentation that was boxed with the software? How could they be gently discouraged from using the telephone?

Then there was the problem of how to distribute incoming calls to the five or so people who made up the tech support team. Should the calls be delivered in grab-bag style, allowing any agent to deal with them regardless of ability? Should certain types of problems be routed directly to the reps who were most knowledgeable in that area? And how could management determine whether some tech support agents took longer than their peers to handle certain types of problems?

In many ways, the solution for PCmusician's first problem resembled the one used by the Harrymore Hotel, just modified a bit. You'll recall that the Harrymore's goal was to direct callers to reservation agents as quickly as possible while entertaining those who needed to wait. PCmusician's callers were also queued, but rather than being entertained while holding, they needed to be informed. So, every minute or two, recordings were played to remind callers of the alternatives available to them—website, email, info line, and so on. Then, after holding approximately five minutes, callers were given the option to record a voice mail message for a callback in the near future.

The second problem was somewhat tougher to solve. PCmusician's first step was to divide its agents into two groups, each of which specialized in different software products. Next, in order to distribute calls to the appropriate group, the system needed to identify which of the company's products the caller was requesting help with. So, immediately after picking up a call, the system played a recording that asked the caller to state the name of the product he used. On the basis of the customer's answer, the call was then routed to the correct tech support team.

To effect the above solution, PCmusician had to employ a phone system sophisticated enough to handle two call flows within one program, or two queues at one time. The system also had to be capable of shuffling overflow calls back and forth between the two support groups in the event one group was idle while the other was overwhelmed.

Lastly, PCmusician needed a system capable of monitoring its queues so management could decide how to staff the help desk at any given time. The managers at PCmusician were aware that there was a direct correlation between the length of time a caller was on hold and the cost of providing technical support. To them, shorter holding times meant that their highly paid support staff was taking calls that the company's website, info line, or email could answer just as well at far less cost to the business.

Therefore, a major function of PCmusician's phone system was to direct callers away from the help desk and, at the same time, present faster and less expensive alternatives to its callers. In the company's view, those customers who really needed telephone support would be willing to make a time investment in order to receive it. In fact, PCmusician considered an hour's wait per caller to be acceptable. If holding time was shorter than an hour, management knew its tech support department was over-staffed.

Technology Recap

PCmusician selected a PBX telephone system that provided the following capabilities:

Phantom extensions

A fictitious tech support extension number (not associated with any specific phone) is programmed to ring on any telephone within the system. In this way, though each agent is assigned an individual extension number for internal and DID calls, all agents can answer the phantom extension.

Automated attendant

Calls to PCmusician's main number are fielded by an automated attendant, which offers the following options: dial the desired extension number (if known), select the dial-by-name directory, transfer to the operator, or choose from a short menu—accounting, sales, technical support. Callers selecting technical support are transferred to the phantom extension.

Universal call distribution

Incoming calls to tech support are first routed to each phone with the phantom extension until the call is answered. If all agents are busy, UCD then plays a recording for callers that offers them the choice of leaving a voice message or remaining in the queue.

Voice mail system

Callers choosing to leave a voice message are called back by a technical support agent, usually within 24 hours.

Call accounting system

PCmusician uses call and extension detail reporting to compare the number of callers dialing its main number and toll-free number with the number of callers actually routed to tech support.

8

Multimedia Call Centers

· ·

EVERYTHING IS GOING DIGITAL. Just think of all the little computer chips that surround us—in our phones, TVs, CD players, watches, appliances, cash registers, even thermometers and blood pressure cuffs! Computerized "whatever" is standard in the United States today. In addition, the Internet has become an increasingly significant force in our everyday lives. Some people theorize that one day every device and appliance we own will somehow be connected to this enormous, global computer network.

Businesses that have relied exclusively on telephone communications in the past must now adjust to the fact that their customers may prefer to contact them in other ways. "What's your email address?" is no longer an afterthought in business conversations. And statements such as, "Our website is under construction," or "We'll have email sometime after the first of the year," only portray your business as sadly behind the times.

Call center technology, of course, revolves around the telephone call. As we have learned, call center management spends a good part of its resources on developing protocols and systems designed to deliver high-quality experiences for their customers.

There are protocols for how interactions take place between agents and customers, as well as protocols for how long a caller may hold or when a voice mail message must be returned. As you'll recall, these rules are built right into the phone system. Other protocols help resolve management issues, such as how many agents to staff for certain times of the day.

When call center managers want to accommodate other types of communications, they face some special challenges. For example, on the surface, it seems like a simple thing to assign email addresses to all the agents in a call center so they can exchange email with customers. However, problems arise when the protocols mentioned above are applied to two different communication methods that exist on two different platforms.

CUSTOMER RELATIONSHIP MANAGEMENT

Technology has come up with a solution, however, in the form of a new type of call center system called either a multimedia call center or a customer relationship management server. Indeed, the term "customer relationship management (CRM)" recognizes the importance of achieving the best possible interaction with a customer at every opportunity.

These systems utilize specially developed, highly customized servers that are capable of providing IVR for callers, ACD functionality, and voice messaging. The same ports concept seen in voice mail is used here, but the voice connections are provided by the ports inside the PC server. In essence, manufacturers have layered various call center technologies one on top of the other and then packaged them all together in one box.

So, what exactly happens when your customers call into a CRM server? First of all, an automated attendant answers the call and offers the caller a self-routing option. If customers choose this option, they are connected to the IVR to access the information they need.

If callers choose to speak to an agent, however, all the stacking and queuing rules of ACD come into play. The system will play recordings asking them to hold, reminder recordings, and, of course, music or advertisements while they wait. Just like ACD, calls will also be distributed evenly among the group of logged-in agents.

Call center agents interface with the CRM server via a window on their PC screens. It shows them all incoming calls, pending emails and faxes, and voice mails for future follow-up. These multimedia queues should be programmed to prioritize the events the agent needs to handle.

For example, voice calls on hold should be at the top of the queue in the order received, or perhaps sorted so that preferred customers are given priority. Ordinarily, email is queued after phone calls. However, if protocol states that email must be answered within four hours, the queue must adjust itself so that unanswered email approaching its time limit is prioritized above voice calls.

Lastly, as soon as an agent takes a call, the CRM system loads the customer's database record so that it appears simultaneously on the agent's PC screen. This is the screen pop feature I have described earlier in this book, and it saves loads of time for a call center's agents. Most importantly, though, it instantly provides the agent with all the information needed to assist the caller.

In the meantime, your supervisors require the ability to reassign agents to different queues. They must also be able to check the status of all pending events, whether voice calls, callbacks, outbound calls, or any other type of call, and reports detailing the interactions between your agents and your customers must

Supervisor's Screen (screen shot)

Supervisors in a multimedia call center have access to statistics on both agent status and queues, plus the details of every interaction pending in a queue.

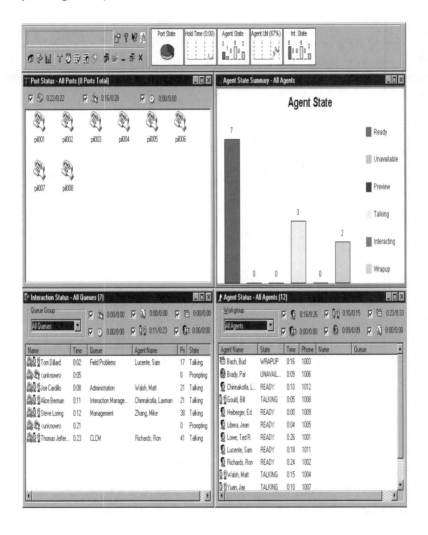

Courtesy of Mitel Corporation (www.mitel.com)

be readily available. A CRM system gives your supervisors all these capabilities directly from their PC desktop displays.

A multimedia call center system includes other features you'll need, too, such as a voice mail messaging system as robust as any stand-alone version. Or perhaps you'd like your agents to dial a list of prospects and customers when incoming calls are slow. Whether new sales calls or follow-up calls, the system can be programmed to present outbound calls to your agents whenever they are free. After dialing each call automatically, the system records the outcome of the call for reporting purposes.

Prior to multimedia call center servers, agents had to attend to email, voice mail, and faxes separately—email on the PC, voice mail via the telephone, and a fax machine somewhere in the building. Management had no control over how agents were balancing their workloads. No doubt some agents did very well and others fell apart, but the call center manager wasn't able to determine who did well and who didn't.

In contrast, a CRM system funnels each agent's workload through one real-time interface located on the computer screen in front of him or her. By using a common set of rules for communicating with customers, all agents are thus able to manage their time and performance in a consistent, measurable way.

Most importantly, when your business has questions about how to meet its various obligations, specific answers can be derived from a reporting system that reaches across all the communications platforms used in your call center.

The price tag
Do you think the call center design I've just outlined is too good to be true? Not so. There are several packages and servers

that can provide all the features I've just described, but can small businesses afford them?

First of all, you must realize that multimedia call center packages require extensive integration into your existing business systems. For example, for your customers to utilize IVR or to provide screen pops for your agents, your databases must be linked to the CRM system. In addition, it may be necessary to link your network to the multimedia call center so that email, fax messages, and phone calls can be passed between various servers to each agent's desktop. It comes as no surprise that this kind of customized design can get quite expensive.

Like ACD and IVR, the price of a multimedia call center is measured in terms of cost per agent or seat, because savings in labor expense is the area where you'll find the dollars to pay for this technology. The actual cost per agent will depend on how many you employ, because the design and installation of a CRM system will be the same whether you have two or 200 agents. In my experience, I have seen the cost of such systems range from $10,000 to $50,000 per agent.

Remember, though, that huge savings in labor resources can be realized if callers have the option to help themselves via an IVR system. Then, factor in the time each agent saves on a call if screen pops are used, not to mention the labor saved by stacking calls during high-volume peaks (rather than putting on extra staff). Also, agents save more time per call by using only one communications program for all customer interactions. Even your management staff will save time by having only one place to go for reporting and system programming.

It's reasonable to expect that implementing such a system could cut your labor expenses by 25 percent. Therefore, if you pay your average employee $25,000 per year, wouldn't the system pay for itself in one or two years? Most businesses would consider that kind of return a very good investment.

The fact that these multimedia systems exist indicates to me that modern customers expect call centers to be able to communicate in a variety of ways. While your business may not be able to install a full-fledged CRM system, be sure to handle all communications media the same way you would a phone call.

First, determine what your customers expect from you in the way of response and turnaround times, and then automate the process if possible. By using tools and techniques from the voice world, you can still deliver a high-quality customer experience that will position your business ahead of your competitors.

BRINGING THE INTERNET INTO YOUR CALL CENTER

Millions of subscribers to America Online are familiar with a handy feature known as Instant Messenger. Though other versions of this technology are certainly available, it has long been a standard for those who connect to the Internet via America Online. Do you use it yourself? If not, let me give you an example of how it works.

A dear friend of mine living here in Phoenix takes advantage of AOL's Instant Messenger to keep in touch with out-of-town family members. Her mother lives in Cleveland and her oldest son is in Washington, D.C., but whenever any of the three happen to be online, they can check to see if the others are available to chat with.

If so, a special window appears on each of their computer screens where they can take turns writing short messages to one another. Because the messages are displayed almost immediately, they can actually converse back and forth, much like a two-way radio.

Unfortunately, to chat this way on the Internet, you and your friends, family, or acquaintances must all have access to the same instant messaging platform, such as that provided by America Online. As a matter of fact, this very problem was the subject of a story I heard on the radio recently.

It seems that at least three different manufacturers of instant messaging software have taken up the challenge of developing a common standard for their products. They estimate that some 20 million computers are already programmed with their software, so a joint standard for instant messaging would allow users on any of these devices to chat with one another in real time. Just think of all those people messaging on the Internet instead of talking on their telephones.

This radio story really got me thinking about the Internet in general. I thought of the dozens of times I have witnessed one or both of our teenage girls typing away on some teen chat line about who knows what, perfectly at ease with this powerful technology. And I thought about all the software manufacturers vying to turn your Internet-connected PC into a telephone. And then I thought about the data network I routinely use to check on the PGA Tour's latest standings or to find out what time the Diamondbacks' next game airs on TV. And, finally, because I am writing this book, I thought, "How will call centers be affected by these increasingly popular ways to communicate over the Internet? "

It's interesting to note that we're not talking about totally new technologies. When I worked as a call center agent back in the '80s, I could use my operator terminal at work to modem to my IBM 8088AT PC clone at home. Then, once connected, I would have a nice two-way chat with my wife even while taking telephone calls.

What *is* new is the proliferation of these technologies. Nowadays, instead of consulting a phone book or a reference at the public library, I'll turn to the Internet first. Likewise, when I need information from a particular business or government office, I'll check their websites before calling one on the phone. I know I'm not alone in using the Internet this way.

We expect a lot from the Internet—we use it to bank, trade stock, stay in touch with our relatives, search for a car, buy a new house, and even look for a better job. Furthermore, those of us who run small branch offices for large corporations know that the Internet has virtually replaced the telephone and traditional mail as the means of connecting to the resources of our parent companies.

So, to return to my question, how are call centers being impacted by Internet communications? Clearly, the same individuals who shop online will want to communicate with you online, too. Customers may want to use instant messaging to chat with your agents about a service issue. Or, perhaps they are using their only telephone line to connect to your website, and now they need to ask a question. Internet-based telephony may be the best option for these customers, but can your center handle the incoming call?

Probably not. This deficiency won't put you out of business any time soon, however. Chances are that only one to five percent of your customers are ready to communicate with you over the Internet in real time, and they can still reach you by telephone if they really want to. Nonetheless, in large call centers handling 10,000 calls per day, one to five percent of the day's calls can add up to a substantial number of lost business opportunities. It's obvious that these call centers need to make sure they can handle Internet communications now.

The rapid pace of technological development today is such that I could never hope to identify all the ways to bring live Internet communications to your call center. No sooner is a product on the market than a competitor comes out with something entirely new and better. So, I am reduced to describing the technology you'll need in the most general terms. That said, let's take a look at what's out there.

Solutions found outside the call center

First of all, there is off-the-shelf software that enables communications between people using the same technology. If you have a limited number of clients who want to use the Internet, you have several options. You could utilize instant messaging, schedule time in an Internet chat room, or purchase Internet telephony software. Whichever option you and your clients choose, you must both agree on the specific system to be used.

Secondly, you could hire a service provider to act as a common clearing house for your communications. For example, a company based in Phoenix will set up your business with both a telephone number and the necessary software to connect you to its server. From there, you can make unlimited telephone calls from its Internet-connected PC to anyone else connected to the same network. As a member of this network, you could point your customers to this service as well. Then, once they download the free software, they'll be able to contact your business online whenever they want to.

Solutions found inside the call center

Think back to the multimedia call centers described earlier in this chapter. Remember how all communications methods were represented and queued on each agent's desktop? Within this environment, I have seen three Internet options evolve for your customers.

The first option allows the customer to establish a two-way chat session (via computer keyboard) with a call center agent. While browsing your company's website, he or she could select a button labeled along the lines of "chat with a customer service rep." Once an agent is available and the chat session is initiated, the customer and agent can communicate real time.

In addition to chatting, agent's usually have the ability to "push" a website location. This is accomplished by software on the call center's end that automatically links the customer's Web browser to the page being pushed. For example, if a customer is confused about how to find a specific page within the company's website, the agent simply selects the appropriate page, hits the "push" feature, and the page comes up on the customer's screen.

One of the drawbacks associated with text-based Web chats is that they take up more time than voice calls. Obviously, it takes longer to type a question than to ask it, and it takes longer for an agent to formulate a written response than it does to just say it. In the end, many call centers may determine that Web chats are an inefficient use of their staff's time.

I have actually dealt with several call centers that implemented Web chat capability only to disable it a few months later because of its drain on their agents' time. Nevertheless, if a majority of your customers have only one telephone line, then allowing them to contact you via the Internet in real time may prove to be a huge advantage over your competitors.
But what about options two and three? Yes, there are alternatives to Web chats that a call center can employ.

Option two is the instant callback, which allows a customer browsing your website to request a callback at another phone number he has access to. These requests are queued on an agent's desktop as priority voice calls, and the call center server dials them automatically as soon as an agent is free. In a moment or two, the designated phone rings and your agent is able to help your customer. Also, if the customer's Internet session is still active, the agent has the ability to push websites to the customer's PC as needed.

Lastly, option three is a simpler version of option two. In this case, callbacks can be requested at a specific time. Let's say your customer is browsing your website at 11:00 at night. He might request a callback on his cell phone between 8:00 and 8:45 the next morning when he knows he'll be sitting in traffic on his way to work.

The price tag of implementing Web communications tools specific to call centers varies wildly. Generally, they are integrated software components of a large, multimedia call center design rather than small, stand-alone software packages. Therefore, almost every application would require manufacturers or developers to customize their products to your company's existing system, all at significant cost.

If integrated into your total call center design, Web-enabled communications become yet another path for your customers to reach you. Quite possibly, it's a way to capture business that other companies are not prepared to take advantage of, but the only real way to justify such an expense would be substantial demand from your customers.

COMPUTER TELEPHONY INTEGRATION (CTI) AND COMPUTER-BASED TELEPHONE SYSTEMS

In 1994, I had just moved to Seattle to work for Tri-Tec Communications (a great interconnect, in my opinion). During my second or third week there, the sales rep for one of the telephone systems we represented stopped by on a training mission. For about an hour, he shared his thoughts and theories on the state of our business and described the newest products his company was offering.

Midway through his presentation (I distinctly remember the moment), he became quite serious. A new wave of technology, known as computer telephony integration (CTI), was rapidly reshaping our industry, he told us. All the telephones we had been installing for the past 15 years would soon be connected to computers, making handsets and push buttons obsolete. Our familiar telephones would be reduced to images on our computer screens.

Therefore, you must become a computer company, he warned us. Soon you will be selling computers instead of telephones, and you will be installing software instead of phone systems. On top of that, this messiah of CTI actually predicted that any company unable to adapt would find itself out of business in less than two years.

It is true that the integration of computers and telephones has significantly impacted those companies that provide telephone and call center technologies. Many of the more sophisticated technologies described in this book are a direct result of CTI's development and would not be available if the computer/software world had not joined hands with telecommunications.

However, it is safe to say that our telephones are still with us in the year 2001, and as far as I know, CTI has not been directly responsible for the ruin of any telephone system manufacturer. The entire technological trend has evolved more slowly than our enthusiastic rep predicted because there was never a tremendous need for this type of sophistication. In the end, it seems customers are more interested in service than revolution.

Traditionally, telephone systems have always been closed proprietary systems. For example, if you want to add features, lines, or telephones to your Toshiba telephone system, only Toshiba can help you. Computers are just the opposite, though. A PC's hardware might be fabricated by any of a long list of manufacturers. In fact, of the 10 or 20 components that make up an entire computer system, it is feasible that no two have been made by the same manufacturer.

Due to these open standards in the computer world, anyone who wants to try his hand at building a computer can do so by gathering the various parts from whichever vendor he chooses. Standards for PC software are also open. Though it wasn't always this way, today most software is written to work with the operating system loaded on your PC. This means that whenever you want to add or change something, nearly any vendor can supply you with what you need.

However, to integrate telephone systems (using proprietary standards) and computers (using open standards), there had to be some sort of interface for them to exchange commands and information. Technology enabling such communication was subsequently developed in two flavors.

Telephone to computer

This technology, flavor number one, links a single computer and a single telephone through a cable connection supplied by the telephone maker. Typically, the phone is connected to the computer via a serial port on the PC, and software is installed to control the telephone.

The software usually depicts some sort of stylized telephone on the computer screen, but in some cases, a more accurate representation appears complete with buttons to click on for dialing or for access to other features of the phone system. When users want to dial a number, the computer sends its commands to the telephone via a Microsoft-developed standard language called telephony applications programming interface (TAPI). This open standard applications interface has allowed software developers to write programs that can work with any telephone system that is TAPI compliant.

More sophisticated applications were also developed, such as the personal information manager software available with ACT! When you click on a contact in your ACT! address book, this program will automatically dial the phone number of the selected contact. In addition, if caller ID is available, the computer can read the number of an incoming call, check it against your personal address book, and bring up your entry for that contact as the call is ringing to your desk. How handy is that?

The telecom industry went wild for a while over such great tools, and some users really bought into the concept. Nevertheless, not enough sales momentum was generated by these desktop productivity enhancements to create the revolution. So, CTI developers were forced to rethink the application of this technology from a different perspective.

Computer network / telephone system

The second incarnation of computer telephony integration was pioneered by Novell with a standard named telephony services application programming interface (TSAPI). Instead of linking an individual PC to an individual telephone, this standard utilizes a physical connection between your telephone system's base cabinet and the Novell computer network server. To dial a number from this environment, you bring up the address book entry you want on your computer screen and click on it. The server then tells the phone system to have your extension dial the selected number. In the same way, all commands from a CTI software application are sent directly from the server to the phone system's base controller.

Perhaps the main advantage to connecting devices at the network level is the more sophisticated level of programming that can be employed. Such programming enables your CTI application to accommodate multiple extensions and multiple lines of traffic simultaneously.

Similarly, management gains the ability to view the phone system's activity as a whole rather than monitoring individual telephone-to-PC interactions one at a time. And, when making routing decisions or selecting features to program, developers can tap the entire network for resources in addition to the databases and programs accessible from each individual PC.

PC-based telephone system

At the beginning of the computer telephony age, industry visionaries foresaw that telephone systems would soon be replaced by computers, forcing phone system manufacturers out of the market altogether. Their thinking was that standard, off-the-shelf PCs could provide telephone line connections, effectively taking the place of a phone system.

Such an arrangement would not only be cheaper than installing a phone system; it would also speed the development of new features due to the rapid evolutionary pace of the PC world. Seven years later, however, two major problems still exist that prevent PCs from becoming phone systems.

The first problem, probably the biggest, is the physical makeup of a personal computer. A standard PC consists of several base components, one of which is the processor—an Intel 386, 486, Pentium, Pentium Pro, Celluron, and so on.

Telephone systems also have processors, but they typically run at much slower clock speeds than the chips housed in our PCs. Plus, there are several of them. In most phone systems, the base processor provides the horsepower for the system. Then, there may be a smaller processor, or switching matrix, to handle connections between incoming lines and stations, as well as another separate processor that handles the load of a T1 line card. A station card running eight telephones may have its own processor, and even a digital telephone set may have its own.

To efficiently process all the traffic a phone system is required to handle, telephone system manufacturers had become skilled at building customized computers. Just think for a moment about your own company's business phone system. What is your tolerance for the timely processing of telephone calls? What would be your reaction if you picked up a receiver and heard dead air instead of a dial tone? Totally unacceptable, right?

Unfortunately, it was quickly found that a standard PC's single processor totally bogged down under heavy phone traffic, resulting in delayed dial tone, hesitations or pauses as line connections were made, and two- to three-second delayed responses when punching the buttons on a digital phone. While PCs are certainly well-suited to handle five or ten tasks at a time, they simply couldn't keep up with 40 simultaneous telephone conversations—an event the most basic phone system can handle with ease.

Problem number two involves the design of PC hardware. Mid-range telephone systems can provide expansion capacity for anywhere from 40 to 500 or more attached telephones and lines. In contrast, the tower PC clone living under my desk for the past four years has only six expansion slots. After adding three peripheral devices—modem, video card, and sound card—three are free to support device cards. Even if I could fit several telephone lines on one card, there's still not enough real estate on my PC to use it as a viable phone system.

This unhappy situation brings us to the subject of phone system software. When PBX and telephone system manufacturers sell you a telephone system, they are not only providing all the necessary physical equipment for connecting telephones to telephone lines; as we've discussed, they are also building a custom computer for your business. The ability to place a call on hold, buttons that flash when a phone rings, and the dozens of other features you may have selected—all are provided via the vendor's proprietary software.

On the other hand, a PC telephone system's hardware is composed entirely of a standard, right-out-of-the-box PC. All the physical connections between your telephone lines and telephones are provided by this PC. However, PCs require an operating system, such as a Windows platform, before they can run any software or perform any task. In effect, then, a PC phone system is only a software program running under Windows NT, for example, or some other operating system.

How reliable is Windows NT? That's debatable, but I do know that it is not acceptable for a telephone system to wait to pull dial tone on your phone while it "thinks" about something. And it is never okay for a phone system to reboot in the middle of the day so that callers have no way to reach your business until the reboot is complete. And it is always totally unacceptable to have your phone system "freeze up" on you in the middle of a phone call.

If any of the above ever occurred at your business, wouldn't you be screaming at your phone system vendor to fix it? Or maybe you'd just rip it off the wall and toss it into the parking lot. The fact is, due to its hardware construction and the reliability of today's operating systems, the pure PC-based phone system is not quite ready for widespread implementation. It is getting closer, though.

In the mid-'90s, a company called DASH put out a respectable telephone system that resembled a tower PC, which, I believe, used standard PC architecture. Mostly, I saw it in smaller offices, but I did spy one that supported about 50 phones in a construction and development company located in Phoenix.

Still, I don't think the proprietary phone system manufacturers face any imminent threat from their PC-based phone system competitors. The Windows NT phone systems offered by many manufacturers seem quite unable to find a market. They are still more expensive than traditional phone systems line by line, and they do not yet offer the types of telephone-based features business users have grown to depend upon. Also, as I have mentioned earlier, the expansion capacity of these systems is severely limited.

What *has* evolved are PC-based phone servers. These add-on servers are peripheral boxes that attach to the standard proprietary systems to provide a variety of call center applications. They also function as database integration links between phone systems and local area networks, or as voice processing servers for IVRs and unified messaging platforms.

Router-based telephone system

I am an optimist. If the market is patient, I believe the PC-based phone system's limitations can be worked out, and I feel sure these types of systems will be successfully adopted in the business world. In the meantime, however, there's a chance that the traditional, proprietary phone system may yet be doomed.

Is it possible that my manufacturer's rep had the right idea, but made a mistake choosing which device would replace the traditional phone system?

There is a piece of hardware routinely found in many businesses that have computer networks up and running. Similar to a telephone system, this equipment was designed and built to accommodate physical connections between stations (PCs) and lines (network segments). Because it has the processing power to run software, it's easy to add a variety of features to its core responsibilities. What could this fabulous piece of equipment be? It's your network router.

Think about it—a router-based telephone system. Cisco manufactures one, and so does Bay Networks. Each company has enhanced its products to the level where voice calls can be integrated into traffic between network points. At I write this book, Cisco has the advantage over its competitors. It is the first company to bring a good solution to the market, and its product is way ahead of anything the PC-based phone system manufacturers have.

The reason for this is that Cisco's base platform is built for the kind of processing and expansion necessary for telephony applications. Clearly, Cisco is already in a position to leverage standard PC architecture. A router is a switch, right? And so is a telephone system. By combining the computer and telephony worlds, Cisco has devised a product that could conceivably replace traditional phone systems on a large scale. So, it appears that my sales rep friend might be right after all—just five or ten years later than he thought.

CTI IN TODAY'S CALL CENTER

While historical background and future speculation are both fun topics to write about, I know you are reading this book to help you with your business needs today. That said, I can tell you that Microsoft's server level, network-based telephony API has become a standard platform for CTI servers. Because it is based on the Windows NT operating system, it is especially appropriate for those businesses already working in a Windows NT environment.

Microsoft offers quite a few call center applications and programs, such as the IVR described earlier in this book. In addition, the multimedia call center application I profiled, some of the reporting tools I've talked about, and the monitoring system I've written about can all be run on Windows NT servers. While we might like to have a little choice in the matter, the truth is that Microsoft's operating system is by far the one most written to for CTI applications.

The difference between proprietary and open computer telephony solutions is an important distinction for you to make. To determine whether the server you want to buy operates on an open or proprietary platform, be sure to ask yourself the following questions:

- Will it work with phone systems other than the one I currently own?

- Can the server's hardware be purchased through your standard PC hardware channel?

- Is it capable of running more than one application? (For example, you may need to run your voice messaging program as well as your IVR platform.)

Also, consider that ease of administration is another huge benefit of open systems. Because of the nature of Windows NT, developed CTI applications are traditionally administered in the same way as a Windows-based program running on NT. All the same organization and application tools that you are familiar with in other server-based applications still apply, such as adding users in directory services or using properties tabs and profiles.

By learning how the CTI server and server-based applications have evolved, I hope you'll have a better understanding of what to look for when it's time to make a purchase. Knowledge is power, so they say, and when it comes to spending your hard-earned dollars or running a successful business, there's no such thing as too much information.

And gathering information is exactly what we're going to talk about in the next chapter.

Applications

· ·

IT SEEMS THAT MOST CALL CENTER problems focus on how to handle incoming calls when they outnumber the personnel available to answer them. Typically, the solutions involve offering callers options to self-direct (via recordings and menu selections), entertainment if they choose to hold, and ultimately delivering the call to an individual or a group based on availability. Reporting features are usually considered a desirable addition to the overall call center design.

Wouldn't it be easier if there was one technology that could solve every problem? Unfortunately, that's not the case. There are at least three technological alternatives just to solve the problem of queuing calls. How to choose the best one for your particular needs will depend on the complexity of your call center and, of course, your budget. With that in mind, take a moment to read about how Needle Food Corporation solved its call center woes. You may recognize its problems as similar to your own.

APPLICATION: INTERNAL HELP DESK

In the late '90s, I had the opportunity to visit Needle Food Corporation's headquarters in Irvine, California. I was there to attend a tour of its extremely sophisticated call center, which was staffed by 15 or so PC software specialists.

These technical gurus manned Needle Food's internal software help desk, where they were responsible for supporting all the software programs running on all the computers in all the offices of Needle Food's empire around the world—a total of about 150 different software applications. (If that was my job, I don't think I could sleep at night.)

Of course, different specialists at the help desk had different areas of expertise. Some were expert in one application, while their coworkers knew all there was to know about other applications. Problems arose when Expert A had to yell across the room to Expert B for guidance, or when Expert C decided to transfer his caller to Expert D—just when the caller thought he was being taken care of.

Other problems surfaced as well, such as how to follow up on callers. For example, if a caller's problem required a bit of research, he might or might not call back to learn the results. At other times, a caller might be asked to try a particular solution and call back if it didn't work. Would he? The help desk needed a way to track these callers and their problems so that there was a history to draw on the next time they called.

Like other technical support groups we have looked at, Needle Food's help desk received many calls asking the same questions again and again. How could the call center deliver this kind of repetitive information without tying up the valuable time of its software specialists?

Most of all, though, the help desk wanted to avoid the inevitable crush of calls that came in on days when a system side server went down, or when Internet service was disrupted, or when any global event occurred that would cause problems throughout the company.

After all was said and done, and every problem was addressed, I believe Needle Food Corporation built one of the best technological call centers I have ever seen. So, let's take a closer look at how this was accomplished.

The system that Needle Food settled on provided many of the same features that other businesses profiled in this book have used, such as queuing incoming callers, entertaining callers while on hold, and distributing calls evenly among its agents. However, Needle Food's new server was capable of a whole lot more.

For instance, the system was programmed to match a certain set of skills with certain agents in order to determine who might be the best agent to handle a given call. First, incoming callers are asked a few qualifying questions to get an idea of what their problem is. Then, once the system categorizes the caller, it tries to deliver it to the most appropriate agent available. If the system's first choice is busy, it actually waits for a minute or two before transferring the call to another available, but less knowledgeable, rep. That's rather sophisticated programming, don't you think?

Meanwhile, the help desk's supervisor enjoys a colorful display on his 17-inch computer monitor that allows him to see when incoming calls start to back up. Whenever he deems it necessary, he can order people back from breaks, tell others to wrap up their calls more quickly, or otherwise do whatever it takes to handle the immediate load—all from his desktop. He can even go into the server's programming to reassign the skill levels of agents on the fly, if that's what it takes to get the calls under control.

To deal with the problem of tracking callers' histories, Needle Food implemented a companion problem-tracking software program. In this way, the help desk could follow a caller's problem, document it, schedule follow-ups, and ultimately produce a report analyzing the problem for future reference.

Because the help desk requires access to a copy of every possible software program running in the field, each of its agents works with a huge, powerful computer. The monitor screens attached to these monsters are cluttered with information and open windows running various programs. Across the top of each screen, a bar displays the next three waiting callers in the queue.

When a call comes in from someone who has called before, the caller's record pops up on the screen simultaneously with the ringing of the agent's phone. (Yes, this is the screen pop technology we've talked about before.) For new callers with new problems, a fresh, clean problem-tracking screen is presented with the call. Either way, this one step alone saves an agent half a minute or more on every call.

Do you remember the one event Needle Food's help desk dreaded most? It was the avalanche of calls that inevitably followed any incident affecting the company's network—a server crashing or a construction crew in the middle of nowhere cutting through a cable that connects half the company's offices.

When such an incident occurred, this problem was addressed by first answering each incoming call with a message that detailed the current problem. Needle Food found that when its "message of the day" was played, fully 60 percent of its callers hung up after one minute. Presumably, their question had been answered, so the help desk was free to answer unrelated calls.

Did I mention that Needle Food's customers can also submit requests by email or fax? Such requests are simply integrated into the help desk's call queue. While the system delivers calls immediately to the agents, email is permitted to wait up to four hours behind phone calls before the system pushes it to the front of the queue.

Last, but certainly not least, Needle Food implemented a reporting system that tracks a call from the moment it hits the phone system on through to its problem resolution, subsequent calls, follow-ups made on that caller's behalf, or any other event that either affected or was triggered by the call.

The reporting system allows managers to determine which callers need them the most or which callers take up the most time. They can also see which agents do well and which need help; which types of problems and software applications cost the most to support; and how well the call center responds to emails, faxes, or other requests for help. In short, managers have a wealth of useful information to help them run Needle Food's call center in the most efficient way possible.

This call center may be the most technologically advanced I've ever seen—and probably one of the most expensive. I estimate that Needle Food paid as much as a quarter of a year's salary for each employee to have the tools he uses, but I am sure the cost is well-justified by the improvements achieved in both call handling and problem resolution. For Needle Food Corporation, technology brought ongoing order and control to the internal help desk of this global concern. What is the dollar value of that?

Technology Recap

Because the PBX telephone system at Needle Food is CTI capable, it does double duty. Not only does it serve as the platform for all voice telephone calls, it also provides the link between each agent's desktop telephone and the multimedia server handling the traffic.

Multimedia server

The multimedia queues are represented on each agent's PC desktop by an independent tool bar located at the top of the screen. A continuously changing list of interactions is stacked beneath the toolbar according to priority, whether voice, voice mail, fax, email, or Web callback requests. To one side of the tool bar, a small display shows agents their daily statistics.

To control traffic flow, management instructs agents to log into the system in one of two modes—either "take" or "force." In take mode, agents select their next interaction from the queue by double-clicking on it; in force mode, the next interaction in line is delivered automatically as soon as the agent is available.

The multimedia server at Needle Food supports the following queues:

- **ACD-style multimedia queue**
  Incoming calls to the help desk are routed by DNIS through the phone system into the multimedia server, where rules on how calls are to be delivered, stacked, and queued have been programmed. Through its CTI link, the server instructs the phone system to deliver the call, and, at the same time, it tells the network application to bring up the caller's database record on the agent's PC screen. The server determines the correct caller by screening ANI information or asking the caller for ID, such as a PIN or trouble ticket number.

- **Email queue**
  Email is queued in a similar way to phone calls, with a required response time of under four hours. When an email reaches the top of the queue, the agent double-

clicks it, responds, and flags the interaction as completed. The entire process is timed and tracked by the multimedia server for reporting.

- **Voice mail queue**
  All message recordings, greetings, and menus are handled by the same multimedia server. Agents may respond to voice mail messages by returning the call (automatically dialed by the server), faxing a reply, or sending an email message. Each of these events is tracked by the multimedia server for reporting.

- **Fax queue**
  Fax capability usually resides directly within the multimedia server. As with email and voice mail, specific timing and response rules are applied. All interactions are also tracked for reporting.

- **Web callback queue**
  Needle Food chose to use Web callbacks rather than Web chatting for Internet integration with its call center. The callback request appears as an interaction in an agent's queue. Once selected, the multimedia server calls the customer back and completes the connection between agent and customer. If the customer's Internet connection is still live, the agent can also push Web pages to the customer's browser.

- **Outbound callbacks queue**
  Sometimes, call center managers may ask their agents to make follow-up calls, such as offering users of a certain software program online upgrades. These outgoing calls are loaded and scheduled into the multimedia server, which queues them just like any other interaction. Special rules for stacking these calls in relation to

other interactions are applied. When selected, agents see the same screen pop data as for inbound calls.

Other features supported by the multimedia server include:

- **Skills-based routing**
  Agents are classified in the server by their ability to handle certain problems. After identifying the nature of a caller's problem via an automated attendant-style menu selection, the server attempts to match a caller with an appropriate agent.

  Even when other, less-skilled agents are free, the server can be programmed to hold the call for a predetermined length of time until the desired agent becomes available. Repeat callers are generally routed to the agents who last worked with them.

- **Message of the day**
  New preambles to the call center's regular call path can be recorded as necessary. For example, Needle Food recorded messages that alerted callers to particular events taking place within the company.

Supervisor desktop
A continuously updated picture of the call center (including queues, agent status and statistics, historical data, and so on) can be set up on each supervisor's PC screen. This desktop software also gives supervisors the ability to manipulate work flow from behind the scenes, such as reassigning skill levels or agent groups when needed.

Reporting package
Needle Food's multimedia server collects raw statistics on all interactions as they occur, tracking them from

the moment they arrive in the server to the moment an agent flags their disposition. These statistics are then funneled into a database that forms the basis of numerous reports. Because the reporting database is an SQL database, off-the-shelf reporting packages, such as Crystal Reports, can be used to pull the data out and present it in various formats.

APPLICATION: CREDIT MANAGEMENT

Some of my favorite people in the world work for American Consumer Debt Services, a nonprofit business that helps thousands of individuals and families dig their way out of debt.

I like to think that few people accumulate overwhelming debt on purpose. Often there are unforeseen circumstances involved, such as losing a job or spouse, or suffering an extended hospital stay. Other people simply can't handle the easy credit offered to them and never see the big financial crash that is looming on the horizon.

Regardless of how debt gets the upper hand, many people in a desperate financial position want to honor their debts, but need help doing so. On the other side, creditors know that collecting a smaller payment and allowing more time for repayment is better than not being paid at all. The last thing they want to see is a former customer turning to the protection of the bankruptcy court. This is where companies such as ACDS step in.

A person struggling with debt can enlist the help of an ACDS credit counselor, who will contact all his creditors for him. Working on his client's behalf, the credit counselor is usually able to negotiate a lower interest rate or favorable payment arrangement with each of the client's creditors. The client then agrees to make a monthly payment to American Consumer Debt Services, which is subsequently disbursed to the client's creditors.

ACDS handles all communication with the creditors, and the client gains the opportunity to rebuild his financial position.

There are various ways to organize this type of enterprise. Consumer Credit Counseling, another company devoted to helping folks manage their debt, has small branch locations in most cities across the country. Clients visit these offices directly to set up repayment programs, make payments, and receive counseling and support.

On the other hand, ACDS uses a call center exclusively. Clients begin, maintain, and complete their relationship with ACDS entirely over the telephone or via the mail. Call center technology has given ACDS the opportunity to serve a huge base of prospective clients—the entire United States—with only a minor investment in infrastructure, namely its one call center.

The ACDS call center employs approximately 150 agents, which makes it a fairly large center. Smaller call centers can learn quite a lot from it, though, because at the core of the ACDS business is a one-to-one relationship between clients and counselors. This situation creates a technological challenge that may be similar to your own.

When a call center receives thousands of incoming calls, how do you ensure that each client is correctly routed to his appropriate counselor? How is a counselor's productivity measured when client interactions occur only via telephone and the mail?

When correspondence arrives from three or four different sources—fax, mail, email, and telephone—how do you make sure all are handled according to company standards and none are favored at the expense of the others? Is there a way to shorten the amount of time an agent spends on a phone call without jeopardizing the quality of the caller's experience?

ACDS needed to solve a number of problems in its call center. The company's first step, however, was to structure its staff into teams, each consisting of ten agents plus one supervisor. In this way, the call center could more easily focus on its various problems. Could your call center be divided into teams?

Next, ACDS took a close look at the types of questions callers were asking. Whenever a call center can determine that a majority of its calls are similar and that the requested information is available in its business database, the whole process of delivering key information can be automated.

ACDS found that most of its clients called to find out if their latest payment had been received or whether a certain creditor had been paid. Creditors wanted the same information. In particular, creditors needed to verify if a client was indeed in the credit repair program. Moreover, once a client's account was established, they checked frequently to make sure payments were being made and that the client was fulfilling his ACDS obligation. It became clear that many callers could get the information they wanted without having to speak to an ACDS agent at all.

When callers did need to speak directly with a credit counselor, ACDS learned that agents spent at least 30 seconds just locating the caller's record in the company's database. In many cases, those 30 seconds constituted up to half of the total length of the call. Imagine how this call center would be impacted if technology was installed that immediately retrieved the client's record as soon as the agent answered the phone.

Ultimately, ACDS settled on a multimedia call center server with a built-in interactive voice response system. This system has significantly helped its call center in a number of ways.

First, all callers are asked by a preprogrammed recording to enter their client number, which is immediately matched to the company's database. Then, the system offers a menu of account information choices depending on whether the database has pulled up a client or creditor record. Clients can check their outstanding balance with a particular creditor, or double check when their next payment is due. Creditors can verify that a payment was received by ACDS.

If the caller's question cannot be answered via the menu choices, the call is routed to the appropriate counselor. Should the counselor be already occupied, however, the caller's name and account number appears on his PC screen in a queue. Then, as soon as he is available, the entire record pops up on the computer screen.

At the conclusion of a call, if an ACDS counselor needs to schedule a follow-up letter or a future callback, the system records the information and posts a reminder at the appropriate time.

These types of follow-up calls are made to both creditors and clients throughout a normal business day. Whenever the load of incoming calls slows down a bit, the reminders appear on the counselor's PC window. The agent simply selects which call he wants to make, and the system automatically dials the telephone and brings up the client's record at the same time.

What about email or faxes? Email that comes in from clients and creditors is stacked just like a phone call, and it is managed in the same queue as well. One difference between email and a phone call is that an email is allowed to wait up to four hours in queue. Phone calls are given high priority. As for faxes, an agent can trigger a fax right from the desktop queue.

Though ACDS made a significant investment to acquire this technology, it is clear that every department in its call center benefits from employing an IVR system. Both clients and creditors can now access account information around the clock every day of the year. When it is necessary for a counselor to become involved, he or she instantly has all the information required to help the caller. Supervisors have gained the ability to monitor the activity of their teams in real time, making it possible to change work flow on demand. And management can pull reports that detail all caller interactions, whether via the automated menu choices or with a credit counselor.

Technology Recap

The ACDS multimedia server is identical to the one at Needle Food's internal help desk. The underlying PBX is different, but the CTI integration to the multimedia server and its use of ANI information to identify callers and DNIS routing for incoming calls is identical.

One of the strengths of this type of server is the inherent option of using all or only part of its capabilities. Because the applications lay together to form a whole, a company can build whatever type of call center it wants.

Multimedia queue

The Web integration, fax, and email parts of the program were not implemented because ACDS saw that it had time to roll in these more advanced applications as business warranted it. However, ACDS assigned other applications to somewhat different uses than did Needle Food, resulting in a totally different caller experience.

IVR

ACDS did implement the interactive voice response application. Next, its multimedia server was tied to the company's AS400 database, which is the repository for all customer information. Then, a screen mapping and keyboard stuffing integration was programmed so that the multimedia server could determine the screen co-ordinates of every database field in a given record.

By opening a session to the AS400 and accessing a certain screen, the multimedia server is able to read off different fields of information to a caller. In this way, both clients and creditors can check the status of accounts, payments, due dates, payment dates, and other information directly over the phone.

Reporting packages

An Internet browser report option is available with this particular multimedia server. It allows password-protected viewing of certain reports over the company's internal network as well as the Internet.   Report requests are run at night at ACDS. By pulling up a report menu Web page on his browser, an authorized employee can read through the data, drilling down to individual calls if he chooses.

In addition to the browser reporting option and the standard reporting package provided by its multimedia system, ACDS also chose to maintain a call accounting system on its PBX. This system was implemented to keep track of all non-call center traffic for the business.

Witness monitoring system

ACDS employs a monitoring system that randomly records telephone calls and screen activity for specific agents. This information is then reviewed by quality assurance personnel, and agent performance is occasionally reviewed with both supervisors and the quality assurance team. Such reviews are the basis for both employee raises and training opportunities.

The witness monitoring system consists of a separate server with a CTI connection to the PBX plus a standard network connection to ACDS's local area network.

In summary

Choosing the correct technology for your call center can be a simple matter if you know exactly how you want to serve or capture your customers over the phone. By reading about the experiences of businesses such as ACDS, it is my hope that you will be able to hone in on the specific improvements modern technology can make in your own call center.

On the following two pages, I have included a sample flow chart of how clients' calls are handled by the multimedia system installed for ACDS. So you won't be confused, let me point out that the three options at the end of page 190 are repeated at the top of page 191. These are not new options; the figures are simply overlapped to indicate the continuation of the chart from the previous page.

Though the print may be a little small, see if you can pick out how various types of media are flowed in this call center. Then rejoin me in Chapter 9, where I'll discuss how technology can help you keep track of everything going on in your call center.

ACDS Client Flow Chart

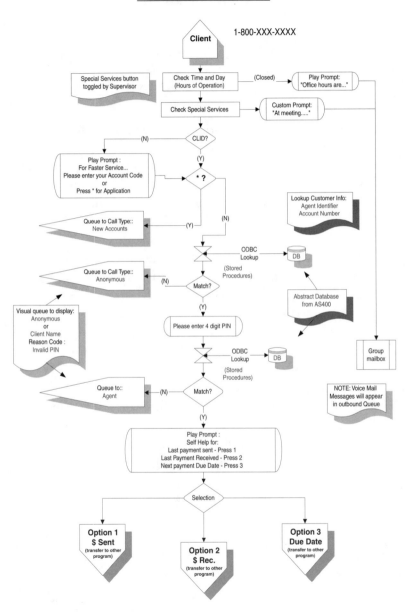

(Continued on facing page)

(From preceding page)

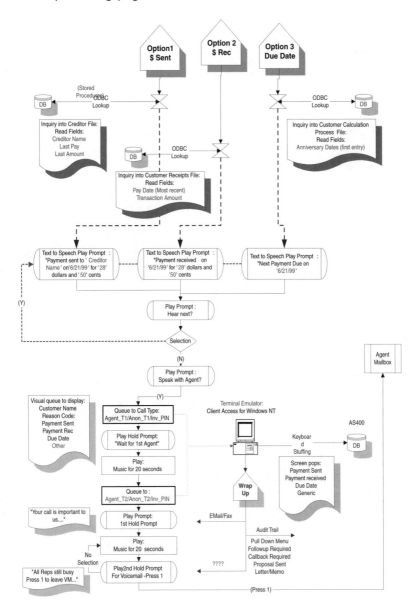

Chapter

9

Keeping Track of Everything

. . . .

HAVE YOU EVER CALLED A BUSINESS that greeted you with a recording similar to this? "Thank you for calling XYZ Company. Your call may be monitored or recorded for quality assurance." In small companies, most calls are neither recorded nor monitored because the effort involved outweighs any benefit to the exercise. In large call centers, however, the opposite is true.

MONITORING

Why do businesses need to listen in on calls between agents and customers? Perhaps the most important reason for monitoring calls is to ensure customer satisfaction. Obviously, a call center has a vested interest in treating its callers well. That's how a business makes money, right? For instance, monitoring calls to the sales department tells managers whether the techniques being used are successfully closing sales. Monitoring calls to the technical assistance department identifies whether its callers' problems are being solved.

There are other reasons to consider, too. Managers of outbound call centers may want to ensure that agents are sticking to their scripts; or they may be assembling a list of objections and opinions from callers to script new responses for. A manager of an inbound call center may question whether a particular customer service agent is conducting himself properly; or he may use his monitoring capability to train new agents.

The folks in charge of training new call center employees know that being able to hear live sessions and then review them with an agent is the most effective way to provide feedback and thus help the agent to improve his skills. Simply sitting your agents in front of a phone with a script will never teach them how to use the most important tools they have—their own voices.

Most agents would prefer not to be monitored, of course. I guess it's only human nature to be insecure about our work performance. While it must be somewhat nerve-wracking to know your boss may be listening to you, the upside is that monitoring tends to keep everyone on their best behavior. And, very often, agents actually need the boss to listen in on a conversation just to witness what is being said by both parties.

In the smallest business call centers that staff only a few agents, managers can assess each agent's habits just by working in close proximity to them. If you're sitting across the room from a guy, you can get a pretty good feel for whether they are working or not. But in a larger call center staffing ten or more agents, it's hard to keep track of everyone.

If a crafty agent is so inclined, he can hide out in a larger group and even manage to manipulate reporting statistics to cover his lack of productivity. Remember the resourceful agent at ACDS who called his own extension to give the appearance of working?

When a human resources manager needs to discipline or terminate such an employee, he can refer to recordings of the agent's monitored sessions to support the action. "Evidence" like this is certainly difficult to argue with, and it removes the unpleasantness of having to involve coworkers, supervisors, or customers.

Monitoring is not just about training or policing agents, though. It can be a valuable aid to an agent as well. For example, how many calls do you think your reps receive from customers who claim they never requested your company's product or service? Your agents can certainly appreciate the value of having voice-recorded verification of orders they placed. And, what about the customer who says he called three days ago to report a damaged shipment? It's a beautiful thing when your agent can quickly pull up a recording of the call in question and then calmly review it with the customer.

Simple monitoring and recording

The most basic call centers consist of just a few telephone stations. Managers of these small centers require only the simplest technology to monitor their agents, especially if the agents are cooperative and monitoring is just an occasional thing. In these cases, a simple way for a manager to listen in on a session is to establish a conference call with an agent before the next outbound call is dialed. By muting his phone's microphone (or just keeping quiet), the manager's presence becomes invisible to both the agent and his client.

On the other hand, business telephone systems typically include a silent monitoring feature as part of the whole package. This feature enables a third party to listen to conversations taking place on any other extension on the same phone system without being detected. It's much the same as eavesdropping on a telephone extension at home.

Recording these line-monitoring sessions is also a rather simple affair. It can be accomplished quite easily with an inexpensive microphone attachment, such as those sold at Radio Shack. Then, suction-cup the mike to your agent's telephone headset and run its connecting wire to a tape recorder on your desk.

Monitoring units and systems

When there are more than just a few lines or calls to monitor and record, you'll want to organize things in a central location. How inconvenient would it be to run from desk to desk, reapplying your microphone's suction cup to the headset of each agent you wanted to monitor? Ridiculous, right? I suppose you could set up a recorder at each desk ahead of time, but if you employ 20 agents, you would need 20 recorders and 20 mikes, plus you'd have 20 sets of tapes to keep track of. I've actually seen this done—in an outbound telemarketing call center seating 300 agents, no less! But, isn't this the kind of clumsiness that today's technology was born to ease?

Specially designed hard-wired monitoring systems can be purchased that consist of little more than a rectangle of printed circuit boards with wire contacts, all enclosed in a metal box. About the size of a child's lunch box, these monitoring units may be wired into either the lines feeding your call center (if copper 1FB lines) or into the extensions themselves (if analog telephone sets). The models I have sold and installed support 20 to 30 stations per box. By dialing a code from a special monitoring phone, supervisors can access any of the devices wired to the box and listen to the conversations taking place on those devices.

An example of a company that uses a monitoring system is Behavior Research Center out of Phoenix, Arizona. This company's expertise is conducting surveys of any kind by telephone, such as political polling, academic surveys, or collecting demographic information. Surveys performed by Behavior

Research Center are highly regarded, and it is frequently cited in the local media as a foremost source for statistical information.

Depending on the individual client, each study or survey undertaken by Behavior Research Center requires different controls and must meet certain standards. To ensure that appropriate controls are in place and that particular standards are being met, supervisors must keep a close watch on their agents. They do so via a monitoring unit manufactured by Malco.

The 40 or so stations in Behavior Research's call center are wired through this unit, allowing supervisors unannounced access to any station. To listen in, a supervisor simply picks up his monitor phone and dials the extension number of the agent he wants to check on. A short beep signals that he is connected to the monitored phone line. At that point, though the agent and the dialed party are unaware of his presence, the supervisor can now hear everything, even the tones associated with one call ending and the next beginning.

Setting up and installing a good monitoring system that covers 25 stations may cost about $1,000, or $40 to $50 per monitored extension. The returns on such an investment include a virtual insurance policy against poor customer service, the ability to offer your agents feedback on their work, and an effective tool for training new hires. I think you'll agree that's a pretty good deal.

What if your company's phone system is digital? No problem. As long as your phone system has ACD call center capability, your business can still reap the same benefits that hard-wired monitoring systems bring to standard telephone environments. Typically, ACD systems provide software monitoring capability as an optional feature set.

Like the hard-wired units we've been talking about, software monitoring is also activated directly from the supervisor's telephone. Agents are not aware of the monitor's presence, and, most of the time, neither is the caller. I say "most of the time," however, because many states have laws against the unauthorized recording or monitoring of telephone calls. In these states, compliant systems must emit a beep audible to both caller and agent that signals when a supervisor is monitoring the session.

CUSTOMER ASSURANCE SERVERS

Even with the aid of the monitoring units discussed in the last section, the job of monitoring and recording calls in a large call center can be a colossal effort, especially when measured in man-hours. If your business requires you to monitor each agent a few minutes per day, or record one or two calls from each agent per week, be prepared to commit significant human resources to accomplish such a task.

My friends at American Consumer Debt Services were faced with just this problem. Because ACDS agents were dealing with credit information and complex issues related to debt, a vital component of the company's daily activity was the monitoring and review of telephone calls to ensure not only proper, but superior, service.

Soon, however, the company's monitoring efforts necessitated hiring two full-time employees, who spent their entire work day cutting into calls, making evaluations, setting up and running recordings, and breaking down the results for reports. At this point, the management at ACDS decided to look for a technological alternative to replace the valuable human resources being spent on monitoring.

Think for a moment about how sound was recorded and stored in the past. Sound recordings used to be archived exclusively as loops of tape on a cassette or reel, but, nowadays, they can also be stored as data files in a computer. Once stored, database software allows us to organize, categorize, and access any kind of recording hundreds of times faster and more efficiently than a tape system ever could. Then, consider how low the cost of a PC hard drive has fallen, plus all the cheap new ways to store data in large quantities—optical disks, removable hard drives, and zip disks, to name a few.

Taking all these technological developments together, a few perceptive and enterprising manufacturers came up with the idea of connecting CTI servers to call center phone systems. In this way, businesses could record every call coming over their phone lines, whether inbound or outbound, and store them to review when necessary.

For example, if it happens to be employee evaluation time, a manager might want to take a look at a given agent's last ten phone calls. Or, perhaps a customer has a problem that he thought was resolved the last time he contacted your business. Being able to refer to a recording of that call will pinpoint any misunderstandings.

Additionally, you could think of this arrangement as an audio security camera, only better. Due to a computer's ability to store, sort, and organize files for access at a later time, this technological setup makes for a very intelligent security device.

The servers I have seen record and categorize calls digitally through the CTI link with the telephone system. Though microphones are on all the time, actual recording begins when each call is connected and ends at the disconnect to avoid storing hours and hours of dead silence. Generally, managers have the ability to monitor calls, while both caller and agent remain unaware of any third party listening to their interaction.

A business might not want to record every call, however. For instance, ACDS programmed its server to record only a certain number of calls for a specific agent within a specific time frame. Because the server communicates with the phone system via a CTI link, it knows when a call starts and when it ends. Therefore, if a manager wants to monitor ten calls from agent Jane Smith this week, the server reads the phone system, notes when Jane logs in for her shift, and records her calls randomly until it has accumulated ten calls in its database.

An advantage to monitoring calls in this random, finite manner is that fewer ports, or voice connections, are required on the system. Also, the amount of space needed on the server's hard drive for database storage is reduced. Both of these factors can contribute significantly to lowering the overall price tag of this type of system.

Screen scraping

Because CTI servers have their roots in the PC world and are necessarily part of a company's network environment, they have the added capability of recording everything that takes place on a PC monitor's screen during a telephone call. Known as screen scraping, this technology works in a fashion similar to film animation. Here's what happens.

First, a picture of the agent's PC screen is recorded by the server (via the network) several times per second. Because of the millisecond timing capabilities of computers today, there is virtually no effect on the real-time images of the terminal screen being recorded. Then, just like a cartoon animation, playback is run in real time at a speed equal to the frames per second recorded. The result is a real-time, moving picture of the agent's screen.

In this way, when managers wish to review an agent's ability to handle questions and situations during a telephone call, they can also see exactly what the agent was doing on his computer at the time. The manager's extra ability to monitor which screens and programs are brought up at which points in a conversation constitutes invaluable feedback for helping an agent to improve his sales or customer service skills.

I experienced firsthand what screen scraping was all about at ACDS. The company's customer assurance and training department had recommended the technology to its president, so an installer by the name of Witness Systems was hired to set the whole thing up.

As soon as everything was operational, the head of the training department tried it out by pulling up a call on his PC screen that had been recorded earlier in the day. Then, as we listened to the agent discussing a specific creditor with his caller, we were able to see every screen change and menu choice he made right on the monitor in front of us.

What an insight into the call! It was as though we had just walked out of an old-fashioned, silent, black-and-white film into a theater showing state-of-the-art, technicolor features complete with Steven Spielberg-type special effects and surround sound. In short, we were blown away. The net effect was the impression that we were right there, looking over the agent's shoulder as he worked.

Not surprisingly, screen scraping is an expensive addition to your family of call center tools. To cover all the agents in the ACDS call center, the cost amounted to better than $1,000 per seat. Like other CTI call center solutions, this technology also requires a great many customized adaptations to ensure the program works correctly for a particular business system. Nonetheless, due to the important role screen scraping played in its call center, ACDS found the cost was easily justified.

In summary, if you are responsible for running a high-traffic call center, and if you must base your day-to-day decisions on the most current and factual information you can get, then screen scraping is the solution for you. Quite simply, it is the best technology available for monitoring at this time.

DISCLOSURE

At the state as well as the federal level, there are laws that govern whether or not you can record a telephone conversation. These laws exist primarily to prevent illegal wiretapping, but they also include provisions for business monitoring.

Typically, the law requires that all parties participating in a phone conversation must be notified that their chat may be recorded. For the systems I have installed in the states of California, Delaware, Nevada, and Washington, a simple preface to the call center queue was sufficient to comply with the law. It was worded along the lines of: "This call may be monitored or recorded for quality assurance purposes." That's all there was to it.

Outbound telemarketing call centers may find notification a bit more difficult. Must an agent tell his potential customer that the call is being recorded even before he gets to pitch his product? That certainly seems cumbersome, and it definitely sabotages the "hit 'em quick" strategy of outbound calling.

However, to be safe, you'll want to consult your lawyer before monitoring or recording outbound calls. The particulars will vary from state to state, so be sure to turn to the proper resources and learn the facts long before your telemarketing campaign is scheduled to begin.

CALL ACCOUNTING SYSTEMS

For smooth call center operations, smart management, and generally getting the most out of your staff and technology, reports compiled from data gathered by your system are the most valuable tools you have. Many of the systems we have talked about feature a reporting component, such as a good ACD system. And, if the makers of multimedia call center servers want your business, they can easily provide you with the ability to generate reports on the status of your call center's activity.

What about smaller companies, though, such as those that don't see enough telephone traffic to support a high-end solution? Don't they need to know how many telephone calls were made from their offices last week? Or, shouldn't they know how much of an agent's ten-hour work day was actually spent talking on the telephone to prospective customers?

Even the smallest business needs to know how many calls come in on its toll-free number, or how many times customers hear busy signals because all lines are tied up. Such information is the only way a company can accurately determine how many telephone lines to install or how many employees to staff in order to catch all the potential business coming its way.

Other necessary reports might include an analysis of long-distance phone bills to determine call counts and their average duration—if you only care about long-distance calls. Local calls need to be considered, too. If you were very enterprising and skillful at your computer, I suppose you could take your phone bill, dump all the data into a spreadsheet application, and then have it calculate averages and totals. However, phone bills appear only once a month, so the oldest calls on your bill are already 30 days old. How useful is that information for making business decisions today?

Call center management decisions tend to center around staffing needs, resource allocation, and technology, all of which require current, up-to-the-minute information. In these cases, your best source for information is a call accounting system. This system may take the form of a stand-alone hardware device or it may consist of software installed on a desktop computer. Either way, a call accounting system utilizes a feature known as station message detail reporting, or SMDR, which supplies a continuous stream of information about every phone call placed or received on the system.

Chances are good that your ordinary business telephone system already supports SMDR. Most commonly, the physical connection between your phone system and a call accounting system resembles a computer serial port on the call accounting end. On the phone system side, it could be anything from a plug to a custom connector that must be wired and attached by the phone system's vendor. However, it is rare that you will need to have your phone system specially equipped at extra cost to output raw SMDR data. Most call accounting systems supply everything you need right out of the box.

SMDR's function is to gather data on each call as it is completed, sort it, and then store it in a database for later retrieval. Such information typically includes the date, time, duration, and phone number of the call. It may also include the extension number from which the call was made, and it may identify which one of your company's phone lines carried the call. In addition, any account codes applied during the call are noted, such as those used by an agent to categorize the call or to bypass toll restrictions. Raw SMDR data is delivered in ASCII text format and can be used to build any number of useful reports.

Generally, call accounting systems are preprogrammed with a set of basic reports, but some PC-based programs allow you to design custom reports. Manufacturers couldn't possibly fashion a program that would accommodate all the ways businesses might want to look at their data. So, these custom report programs are invaluable for addressing any question that comes to mind.

For example, your business may want a report that looks at all calls lasting over one minute and twenty seconds. From this information, you could estimate how many times your agents got past the first question in their telemarketing script. Then, you could compare the number of calls that made it past the first question with the numbers of sales for that day. Wouldn't such a report give your company a good idea of your agents' ability to close sales calls?

Call accounting systems are also great for predicting and allocating the costs of telephone calls. In fact, this was the primary reason that call accounting systems came into being. Hotels, in particular, first used these systems to calculate the cost of telephone calls made by their guests. Later, other companies, such as law firms, adopted the system to charge back the cost of telephone calls made on their clients' behalf. In both these situations, waiting for a phone bill to arrive is totally impractical. Imagine trying to collect a telephone charge from a guest that stayed in your hotel 45 days ago!

Call accounting systems can be a great tool for other businesses as well. In addition to predicting telephone charges, they can be used to audit a company's telephone bills against calls actually made or for divvying up telecom expenses fairly among different departments or individuals within your business.

Fixed-system call accounting

Hard-wired call accounting systems are actually computers about the size of a cigar box that you connect to one of your office printers. Usually, a small keypad and a liquid crystal display are included with these systems in order to access a menu on the display and select a preformatted report.

Hotels are the biggest users of hard-wired systems because they have the memory capacity to hold thousands of calls and are simple to run. Both of these factors are especially important to the hotel industry due to its 24-hour, on-call nature and the tendency for staff turnover to be high. Reports available on hard-wired systems have been largely standardized since hotels began installing (and profiting) from telephones in their guest rooms. The price tag for these systems can run anywhere from $1,500 to $5,000 or more, depending on the storage space needed and the options that are chosen.

PC-based call accounting

There are perhaps 200 or so PC-based call accounting programs available today. Storage capacity of many of these systems is limited only by the size of the hard drive of the computer they are installed on. Much of this software also permits the design of custom reports. You may need to learn a special reporting language to generate anything more than a standard report, but that is certainly a reachable goal for a computer-savvy person willing to invest a small amount of time.

Furthermore, getting to know your system more intimately can be well worth your time in terms of good, old dollars. You'll avoid being a slave to your vendor and his labor charges, and you can choose to glean the most from your investment by knowing how to tap its full potential.

In addition to gathering data on telephone calls, many PC-based systems have modules that can track the usage of your telephone lines. By combining the data collected on both calls and lines, a report can be built that will help you determine how many lines your business actually needs. It may be that your company could afford to drop a line or two. Or, if a report clearly shows that all your lines are busy for extended periods at the same time, it's probably time to add a few more.

Call accounting systems run 24 hours a day because data is only pulled off a call once—right after it ends. If the data isn't collected on the spot by a call accounting system or a specially installed data buffer, it is lost for reporting purposes. This situation posed a problem for the installation of early PC-based call accounting systems, because the software was originally written for DOS operating systems. DOS systems run only one program at a time, so any business wanting to take advantage of a call accounting system was forced to supply a dedicated machine for it.

Some of the old DOS software is still around, but today's call accounting software is written for a Windows platform. Most Windows-based call accounting systems operate by running a small program that collects raw SMDR data from the phone system and stuffs it into a database. This program runs quietly in the background, leaving the computer free to handle any other applications. To generate a report, the reporting and database package is launched from the desktop, and—bingo!—you're in business.

Software packages such as these sell in the neighborhood of $1,000 to $2,500. Yet, in every sale I have made, the customer has still provided a dedicated computer for the program to run on. Unless your company has an old machine ready to be taken out of commission, the purchase of another computer will add about $1,000 to the total price of the system.

We have covered a great deal of material in this book so far, and it's possible that you now know more than you ever wanted to about call center equipment and technology. Nevertheless,

I'm sure you'll appreciate your newly acquired background knowledge as we move on to examine how everything fits together—the subject of the last section of this book.

Section III

Building and Implementing Your Call Center

Chapter

10

Putting All the Elements Together

· ·

WHEN DO YOU NEED CALL CENTER technology? Here are three possible reasons for purchasing some of the systems described in this book:

- When your calls come in spikes, meaning more calls are coming into your office than there are people to handle them

- When your major sales and marketing efforts are exclusively by telephone and you need to maximize every moment on the phone in order to leverage the opportunities you are pursuing

- When your customers can be helped in a generic way using scripts and other standardized methods of interaction

As you begin the process of assembling your call center, consider the story of Insight.com and its huge, stadium-style call center, which receives inbound calls and makes outbound calls in pursuit of mass market sales. Is Insight's need—feeding generic incoming sales opportunities to a staff of ready sales agents—similar to yours?

Or, look at the smaller, inbound technical support staff at PCmusician. This company wanted to give all its customers access to a group of highly trained technical support people, but it couldn't afford to hire extra staff or install more phone lines. Is this your challenge, too?

You'll also want to recall the agents of the outbound telemarketing center I described, who struggle to spend as many working minutes as possible actually talking to live prospects. Is this how you make your living?

Or, perhaps your business is thinking of opening its marketing strategy with a nationwide telemarketing campaign. You can learn a great deal from the folks who do it every day.

Whatever your needs may be, it's time to look at specific ways of leveraging call center technologies to the advantage of your business. Even if you have already decided what is needed, please don't skip the next pages. Although your technology questions may have been answered, there's more ground to cover before making final decisions about the makeup of your call center.

First, discuss your plans with your staff. Because your employees have been interacting with your customers directly, they probably know a lot more about them than you do. Let them help you answer questions such as these:

- Why do your customers call or contact you?
- What do you need to know from them when they call?
- What do their calls represent for your business? Potential sales? Opportunities to satisfy and retain your valuable customers?
- What do you think the ideal experience should be for your customers when they call?

Next, I suggest you map out how a typical telephone call is handled in your business today.

- What happens when the phone rings?
- How many times does it ring, and who answers?
- Is the call held or transferred in any way?
- Does your customer have to wait while you access information for him or her?
- Is there any follow-up to a call, or should there be?

And, finally, solicit input from your staff. Ask them:

- When the phone rings, is it loud?
- When a call comes in, does it ring on every phone?
- How do individuals get calls meant specifically for them?
- Are callers transferred or just parked on hold?
- Are the necessary tools and information needed to handle a call located near their phones?
- Are printed records or documents readily at hand or easy to access electronically?

If yours is an outbound call center, map out a call to a prospective customer. Calculate some averages and ratios, such as a comparison between the average number of calls made and the actual number of prospects spoken to. Then, compare that number with the actual number of sales made. You'll also want to figure in the time eaten up between calls plus the time your agents spend listening for calls to ring through.

Once you have all this information in front of you, you'll have a better idea of where you can improve your callers' experience with your business. Likewise, you'll be able to see which technologies you can employ that will make an immediate impact on your staff's effectiveness. With a clear vision of what you want to accomplish, it's time to move to the next step.

SHOULD YOU USE AN OUTSIDE SERVICE?

If the task of putting together a first-class call center for your business seems overwhelming, maybe the best thing to do is to find someone to help you. Consider outsourcing your call center operation. This concept has become pervasive in business today. Basically, it means you hire another company to take over some function of your business for you, and in the U.S. alone, there more than 100 companies willing to do just that.

Everyone does it. All kinds of activities are outsourced to other companies that specialize in performing a particular task. Because these companies use expensive, state-of-the-art technology and equipment, chances are they will actually do your job better than you could—and for less money.

For example, I recently bought a Canon color printer for my home office, which came with a $30 rebate coupon. Canon doesn't take care of the rebate request itself, but hires an outsourcer to take the requests, process and verify their authenticity, and then prepare and send out the rebate checks.

Various companies I have worked for also used outsourcers to help find and recruit employees, produce Web-based sales training material, manage websites, and prepare and distribute payroll checks. Most newspaper subscription sales are performed by outsourced telemarketers. In the direct mail marketing industry, there are all kinds of companies that will produce and mail marketing materials for you. The list goes on and on.

Successful outsourcers seem to have a knack for finding a definite, separate function that is common to many businesses—something time-consuming, or very *un*specialized, or labor intensive. They then create a large operation that can serve 50 or more companies with a similar need. Many call centers, inbound and outbound, fit this mold.

Some examples of programs handled by outsource call centers include dealer locators, where agents direct callers to the nearest business location, as well as market research surveys, telemarketing campaigns, and catalog sales. For catalog sales, outsourced agents will sell directly from your catalog. Your company then fulfills the order. Outsourcers also process claims requests for insurance companies.

When you mapped out your inbound or outbound caller experience, did you find that it could be simply defined? If that's the case, and if you can develop a standard script that anyone with reasonable intelligence and telephone skills can successfully handle, then outsourcing may be an excellent way for your business to take full advantage of today's call center technology.

The financial argument

Because it contracts with many clients, an outsource company can afford to build a large call center and keep it staffed with agents and support personnel. It can also invest in high-end technology and solutions that you might not be able to afford yourself. This means that it may cost less to have your company's call center built within an outsourcer's facility than it would be to build it yourself.

Consider the cost of space and furnishings. To do it yourself, first figure out how many agents you would need, and then plan on purchasing a desk, chair, and computer for each, not to mention the floor space to accommodate their work area. In addition, you must supply everything else the agents will need to handle the calls coming in, such as catalogs, for example. What would it cost per employee to fund all of this? Outsourcers bear all these costs and build them into their charges to you.

Then there's the technology. What would it cost to outfit each of your agents with the tools we've discussed in this book? To attract a variety of clients, outsourcers use a wide range of the latest technologies, such as predictive dialers, IVR systems, and multimedia call center servers. This type of technology may represent a huge cost consideration for your company, but for the outsourcing company, it is a competitive necessity.

What about the cost of your agents themselves? What wages will you pay? And do agents receive a commission or some kind of incentive pay based on their performance? When adding up potential labor expenses, don't forget to add 30 percent to cover benefits and payroll taxes, plus the time it takes to train a new hire. You'll also need to figure in the cost of replacing agents in the event of illness or abrupt termination. How much business would you lose (in dollars) if two out of your three call center agents got sick on the same day?

Again, outsourcers serve multiple clients, so their staffing expenses are amortized across all the campaigns they are running at any given time. The effect of any sickness or termination expenses is also greatly diluted because of the large number of agents employed. Keep in mind that an outsourced call center makes money only when its agents are working for clients at the billed hourly rate. Therefore, all internal staffing issues are carefully managed to ensure little or no impact on the outsourcer's business .

Lastly, we have to consider the intangible costs of setting up a call center. What price can you put on the knowledge and experience necessary to run a successful call center? Most outsourcers have a great deal of experience working on all sorts of programs that they are willing to share with you. They have already been down the learning curve, encountering nearly every issue imaginable along the way. It's a pretty good bet that an outsourcer can both speed up and improve the process of leveraging call center technology for your particular business.

What you will pay

In addition to the hundreds of U.S.-based outsourcers available, there are companies with call centers all over the world ready to serve you. For example, many Canadian outsourcing companies are looking for your business, and you may be able to hire them less expensively than you could a U.S. company. This is the result of two factors: (1) a higher unemployment rate than ours, and (2) the generally lower cost of building and staffing a call center in Canada.

Costs will vary, naturally. After an initial evaluation, many outsourcers will ask your company to draft a detailed outline of your program so that a price proposal can be determined. I am familiar with three price structures, but I'm sure there are many more.

Most commonly, your company will pay by the hour for the outsourcer's agents. This price structure works best for outbound calling programs, where calls are going out one after the other with little interruption. In these cases, time can be measured in blocks for billing purposes.

On the other hand, I have seen outsourcers charge by the call for inbound service. Typically, there is a variable per-call charge that depends on the complexity of the interaction. In rare circumstances, due to the liability assumed by the outsourcer, a call center will take on a program solely for the per-sale commissions it can generate.

Per-unit costs can usually be reduced by committing to certain minimum levels of volume or to a specific duration for your program. Larger call centers tend to want longer minimum commitments in order to justify the cost of taking on a new client. Nonetheless, there are numerous smaller call centers that will serve businesses with more modest programs.

If you decide to investigate outsourcing, be sure to take a look at the appendices I've included at the back of this book. There, you'll find a list of publications and organizations that can help you find the best outsourced call center for your specific application.

There are many situations where outsourcing is *not* appropriate. At the top of the list may be your company's need to control the call center, its agents, and the information being given out over the phone to your customers. In fact, control may be the most compelling reason to keep your project at home.

Outsourcing is also not appropriate if your intention is to see your business grow with just the people at hand; nor is it meant to take the place of setting up your own call center. Indeed, if communication with your customers is too complex to script and define for a generic call center, then outsourcing is definitely not for you.

In addition to the considerations just mentioned, a careful cost analysis might show that your business is better off keeping its job in-house. What to do? Build your own call center, of course.

ORGANIZING A SPACE FOR YOUR CALL CENTER

Assembling a new call center involves many diverse tasks, each with its own specific requirements that result from your company's unique circumstances and needs.

The physical location

Where do you put a call center? If it's small, it will most likely fit in your existing space. Brand new, larger call centers should be located wherever your labor pool is concentrated.

The typical profile of a good call center agent describes a relatively young, reasonably intelligent, and technologically savvy person. Very often, these agents come from a general labor pool and are willing to work for less money than other groups of employees. That fact might explain why many call centers are located near high-density college towns or in cities with higher unemployment rates. Phoenix, for example, makes a good call center town because it features a mix of both labor pools. (Incidentally, Phoenix also has the highest ratio of call center seats per capita in the nation.)

We can learn from those who have gone before us. Keep in mind that the interactions between call centers and their customers take place entirely through an electronic medium (usually the telephone), so there is never a need to impress anyone with the location of a business or its physical surroundings. Generally, you will not see a call center in a downtown district, a high-rise office tower, or in any "Class A" real estate building. The cost of the operation simply doesn't warrant it.

So, where do existing call centers tend to be located? Most often, you'll find them in neighborhoods close to the labor pool, housed in buildings such as converted grocery stores or built-out warehouses.

Parking is always a concern. Most buildings erected for general business must supply a ratio of four parking spaces per 1,000 square feet of floor area. Large call centers, however, can seat quite a few agents in 1,000 square feet, so the number of available parking spaces may need to be doubled or even tripled. This is probably why some of the largest call centers in the country are actually located in converted shopping malls.

American Consumer Debt Services is a good example. Its call center is housed in a sprawling, single-story, wide-open structure that used to be a suburban shopping mall. Because the mall was designed for heavy retail traffic, it is conveniently located near freeways and boasts a high ratio of parking spaces to building area. Therefore, parking is never a problem for either ACDS or its mall neighbors. In addition, ACDS enjoys huge chunks of space at a relatively low cost per square foot. While I don't know the circumstances behind the mall's conversion to office space, it certainly works for ACDS.

Working environment

A call center has special workplace dynamics. Most people working for other types of businesses are not glued to one place all day. Their working experience is probably a lot like mine. I am not chained to my desk, and I have opportunities to get out and move around. I go out on appointments or down the hall to consult with workers in another department within my company. I may even travel on business from time to time.

Call center agents work under unique conditions, however. They are asked to sit in a restricted space for a full day, every day, and transact the business of your company through strictly electronic means.

Like all other industries, working conditions for call center employees are overseen by a variety of federal and state regulations. But, I trust your good common sense can see that fostering a truly productive environment for your call center team requires some special considerations.

Work space

OSHA and state regulations dictate many workplace standards, such as how high a desk surface should be, what adjustments chairs need to have, how keyboards should be placed, and other ergonomic considerations. Rather than trying to figure out all the pertinent rules on your own, you may find it easier to use the services of a space planner. These people will be familiar with all the requirements mandated by your city and state.

An example of a space planning company is The Linch Company here in Phoenix, which is owned by a friend of mine. This business buys modular office furniture from companies that have either outgrown theirs or have shut down altogether. It is then remanufactured for new spaces. After studying the floor plan of your call center, these types of companies can make specific recommendations on how to arrange both your space and your furniture. Space planners will ensure that your facility complies with government standards, and they can also show you how to make optimal use of your work space.

At American Consumer Debt Services, the workstations are set up in rows. This arrangement is typical of most call centers. The setup at ACDS features 22 rows consisting of 10 workstation cubicles each. At the end of each row is a single modified cubicle, somewhat wider than the others, that faces the row like a coxswain's seat on a 10-man racing scull. This is where the supervisor sits to oversee the team of agents.

You may be familiar with McLeodUSA, a competitive local telephone company headquartered in Cedar Rapids, Iowa, that provides service in 25 states. I'd like to describe McLeodUSA's call center to you, because I think it is a great example of what a call center should be.

For starters, McLeodUSA divides its agents into two groups—an inbound group and an outbound group—and seats them in different parts of the same building. The inbound group consists of McLeodUSA's customer care agents. They answer all incoming calls from customers with questions or problems. The outbound group is the telemarketing side of the call center, which chases business in all the cities McLeodUSA serves.

The floors of the building housing this call center have been treated with antistatic matting. Natural light streams in from numerous windows, and plenty of fluorescent lighting is provided as well. Great care is taken to keep temperatures in a comfortable range, and the technique of pumping white noise throughout the building is employed. Why add white noise when you already have 2,000 or so people all talking in the same open space? Science has demonstrated that raising the level of background noise humans can ignore effectively masks more distracting noise. Interesting, don't you think?

Each of the agents in Cedar Rapids sits in a prefabricated modular booth with a desktop PC and printed reference material close at hand. The space is designed not only for the tools of the job, but it also allows room for displaying the knickknacks many of us like to bring in to personalize our workplace.

These prefab cubicles use floor space very efficiently. Most measure only four to eight feet wide. Another important feature of these modular cubicles is the construction of the dividing partitions. A special sound-baffling material is used, which is an obvious need in any call center—even with white noise!

Amenities

One of eight agents seated in a row of cubicles answering calls for an eight-hour shift—I've been there. It isn't as easy as it might appear. In particular, there are two situations where this type of work can get tough.

First, when incoming calls are slow, the job is tedious. I speak from experience. During my stint as a call center agent, there were periods when there was absolutely nothing to do. Sometimes it was a real struggle just to stay awake.

We couldn't leave our desks, because another call might come in at any moment, and we weren't allowed to making personal phone calls. However, it was OK to play music during quiet periods, read at our desks, or eat snacks. Occasionally, we might be asked to do other types of work, such as stuffing envelopes or reorganizing files. But, overall, slow days could be brutal.

At the other extreme, this job can be tough when calls are flooding in without a break. We all felt an intense pressure to keep on answering right through normal break times and even our scheduled lunch breaks. In the call center where I worked, we typically received an overwhelming volume of calls early in the weekend. At these times, after working my eight-hour shift, I would go home and collapse in bed as if I had been digging trenches all day.

On more balanced days, though, my choice of work only bit into my life in a minor way. Because an agent simply cannot leave his desk or make personal phone calls, it was difficult to take care of those day-to-day chores that have to be done during normal business hours.

Under these circumstances, company-provided amenities can make all the difference between having bored, stressed-out employees or balanced employees, who enjoy their work as much for the environment as for the task itself. Let's face it—no one looks forward to talking on the phone about the same thing over and over for eight straight hours every day!

Among many businesses today, there is a growing trend to provide amenities for employees. Such amenities are seen as a way to foster camaraderie and to add an element of fun to the workplace. For example, I know of at least three Internet companies located here in Phoenix that have set up game rooms with pool and ping-pong tables.

Some companies have gone even further. Active Voice, a voice mail system manufacturer in Seattle, Washington, decided to build a slip-and-slide between two floors and position a digital camera to record the action live. The camera fed into the company's website, so everyone could watch the fun. Unfortunately, the slide had to be taken out of service after while. It seems a few employees became fond of taking huge running starts to see who could hit the wall at the bottom of the run the hardest.

At McLeodUSA's Cedar Rapids office, there is a full cafeteria where employees can grab a variety of snacks or lunches without leaving the building. There is also a gym plus an outdoor walking and exercise area, complete with a small lake. At American Consumer Debt Services, an agent's dry cleaning can be picked up at the office and returned a couple of days later. At this call center, there's a break room with tables, chairs, and deep couches. It's a quiet, comfortable place away from the main work area where agents can truly get away from the job for short periods.

For a small call center, the cost of building a gym out back to attract agents probably can't be justified. But, keep in mind all the little things that a completely desk-bound employee cannot do. Call centers are unique work environments, and they should be treated as such. It's not too hard, really, to think up economical ways to accommodate your agents.

How can an employer make eight hours in a chair more tolerable? What about some of these ideas:

- Provide shuttle service to and from day care
- Install a microwave and a refrigerator in a break room away from the phones
- Provide top-quality chairs
- Set up a ping-pong table
- Install an espresso maker or slush machine

- Bring lunch in for everyone on Fridays
- Start a library of books and magazines
- Fill slow periods with other kinds of work
- Arrange fun competitions, such as shooting baskets for prizes when agents reach certain goals
- Ring a bell whenever an agent closes a sale

Anything an employer can do to make a workplace more enjoyable is greatly appreciated by employees, and the payoff for the company is higher productivity and less turnover.

STAFFING YOUR CALL CENTER

I wouldn't presume to tell you who to hire for your call center or how to go about it. However, I'd like to pass along some call center industry averages that might be enlightening and a few notes on the hiring practices of larger companies. Much of this information is fairly general and somewhat more relevant to inbound call centers than other types.

The average, full-time, frontline call center agent makes about $25,000 per year, working 40 hours per week. If a call center does business nationwide, it is better if its agents do not have regional dialects or accents. This is one reason why large cities—Phoenix, Denver, Las Vegas, Los Angeles, and Chicago, among others—are good locations for large call centers.

However, if you do business within a specific region, it is usually better to hire agents from the community served. Because they will be familiar with all the region's linguistic quirks, callers will be more comfortable talking to them. Foreign language capability is sometimes an issue, and some call centers offer a modest premium to the annual salary of those agents possessing foreign language skills. When the need arises, most call centers simply utilize the foreign operator translation services available from carriers such as AT&T.

There is no one-size-fits-all type of agent. I've seen agents of all shapes, colors, and sizes. So let's not get ourselves into trouble with stereotypes of any kind.

On average, the education level of call center agents is high school plus some college, but they are usually not college graduates. Large call center hiring practices emphasize intelligence without requiring a specific degree. More highly valued than a college degree is a combination of some college-level study plus a solid work history. For businesses that depend on their reps to occupy telephone stations and communicate with customers all day long, a demonstrated ability to show up and do the work is vital.

Many call centers give applicants aptitude tests in an attempt to predict desirable personality traits, such as good judgement and integrity. These traits are often much more important than education, because they relate directly to how agents will interact with customers. Profiles derived from aptitude tests can help to determine which applicants are best-suited to the various customer service functions in the call center.

Most call center agents do not see their jobs as permanent, and that's reasonable. This kind of work is rarely a lifetime goal. Often, the call center job is a stepping stone to a better job, perhaps at another company. Or the agent may see his job as a path to advancement off the floor and into a managerial position within the call center. Others find answering phones to be a good way to make money while in school.

Whatever the case may be, most call center employees view their jobs as temporary, and this attitude has created a huge problem in the call center industry: turnover.

Turnover rates are somewhere between 30 percent and 60 percent per year at small and large call centers alike. Think of all the job advertising, screening, testing, interviewing, hiring, and training that goes on—repeated over and over again. Turnover is the single largest challenge to adequately staffing a call center, and many businesses are trying a variety of strategies to reduce it.

Some companies use more screening tests to weed out unsuitable applicants before they're hired. Others are committing to upward mobility schedules for new agents, offering them advancement after a specific time period. Almost all employers are attempting to make the workplace as pleasant as possible by providing the amenities we discussed earlier.

In frustration, many call centers are using staffing services. Believe it or not, there are staffing services that focus solely on temporary or permanent call center hiring.

The first hiring decision

The people most qualified to communicate with your customers may already work for you. If so, they will be the first people to staff your new call center. If you do need to hire additional people, however, you'll want to be aware of some of the problems that plague all call centers. Having worked with several call centers during my career, I have learned one or two things about hiring new agents. So, allow me to share a few things with you.

Profiling

First define the underlying skills that are necessary for an agent to represent your business. If you hired someone to work at a walk-in customer counter for your business, what would he need to know about your products, services, and procedures? What kind of overall industry experience would he or she need? How would you want your rep to treat and interact with each customer that stepped up to the counter?

The answers to the preceding questions will form the basis of a profile for the ideal employee. Creating such a profile allows you to concentrate your search efforts on those applicants who meet your criteria. Then, when interviewing candidates, the profile will help to keep you focused on the things that are important to you.

Write down the criteria you are looking for—age range, job history, aptitudes, education, and social skills. Be careful not to profile so narrowly that you limit your potential labor pool. Keep in mind that this is a guideline to help you focus your search and not an inflexible blueprint. Sometimes taking a chance on an unorthodox candidate can work out well.

Solicit applicants and qualify, qualify, qualify

We have been enjoying a good economy in recent times with low unemployment rates. Unfortunately, these good times have caused a bit of a problem when trying to staff a call center. Hiring is more of a selling job than it used to be. I remember advertising for call center agents in the mid-1980s. Back then,

I had the luxury of selecting the two or three best-qualified individuals from a field of 50 to 75 applicants! Today, you have to actively search for applicants, and then you have to sell them on the idea of working for you.

Consider using the tools of the marketing business. Advertise, yes, but also consider other efforts, such as job fairs or posting notices at local college campuses. Instead of a classified ad in your community newspaper, use a separate, larger print ad, and don't overlook any other periodicals that your labor pool reads.

Make proactive contacts. Call on business associates, vendors, customers, friends, and family to spread the word about the kind of employees you're looking for. In short, do anything you can think of to expand your choices beyond those persons answering a classified ad. Then, once you have assembled a pool of applicants, remember this salesperson's mantra—qualify, qualify, qualify.

I have sold telephone systems and services for many years. To create opportunities to sell my products or services, I have networked, advertised, direct mailed, and cold-called my way into thousands of sales opportunities.

Nonetheless, I was never willing to invest even an hour of my time trying to make a sale until I determined whether the customer had a real need for what I was selling. In addition, my customer had to be open-minded to my proposal with the resources to pay for it, plus he had to be person within his company who could make the final decision. If left unqualified, these are the areas where many sales opportunities are lost.

The same principles can be applied to your job applicants. You don't want to hire someone and absorb the cost of his training, only to discover insurmountable flaws that could have been detected with proper screening.

Go back and match the applicant loosely with your profile. Then, arrange an initial interview by telephone so you can measure your prospect's ability to handle the telephone. Is he courteous and friendly with you? Can she answer questions in a timely way and frame her responses intelligently?

Next, test your applicant's aptitude thoroughly with one of the software programs currently available for this purpose, or hire the services of a company such as Talent+ and Align Mark. These outfits offer software or interactive voice response solutions designed for testing the aptitude of call center applicants.

An excellent article on the subject of employee turnover and ways to avoid it was featured in the online edition of *Call Center Magazine* ("Leaping Into New Labor Pools" by Brendan B. Read, posted on callcentermagazine.com 04/01/00). It includes examples of software programs that can be used to test the aptitude of prospective agents.

Brendan Read, the article's author, writes, "DDI's (Development Dimensions International) online screening software, Web Screen, gives visitors to your website the opportunity to find out about available jobs at your call center and the qualifications for them. The software displays questions to gauge the aptitude for a specific position and prompts them to schedule in-person or phone interviews."

Read's article also suggests: "There are tests you can purchase to help you screen applicants effectively, including those who have minimal work experience. One of these tests is Stephen A. Laser Associates' (Chicago, IL) 'Ready-to-Work?' which measures attributes like dependability, conscientiousness and emotional maturity. The software determines an applicant's communication skills and ability to operate successfully within a group."

By the way, Read has written a great resource for companies dealing with new call center issues. You can get a copy of *Designing The Best Call Center: A Complete Guide For Location, Services, Staffing, and Outsourcing* (Computer Bookshops, January 2001) at local bookstores or online through CMP Books at www.telecombooks.com.

Lastly, I would like to suggest an ingenious practice that my current employer has adopted for screening applicants. Send your prospects to lunch with a group of your other employees. Let their future coworkers tell you whether they will fit in.

This practice can benefit your business in two ways. First, you get another look at your applicants from a totally different perspective (one more look can't hurt). Secondly, if hired, your new employees will already be accepted by the coworkers who helped to make the choice. Now your call center team has a vested interest in seeing that the new employees succeed. How valuable is that?

Or use a staffing service
Never forget that there is an entire industry built upon the premise that you may be too busy with other issues to find and qualify new agents for your call center. If these staffing services can demonstrate that they have the skills to comb the labor pool for suitable prospects, and if their commission or fee can be justified, consider a staffing service as an option.

The final justification may lie in the number of agents you need. If your call center is to be staffed with 20 or more agents, you'll need to establish an ongoing process for attracting and hiring agents. You may be better off doing the hiring in-house, appointing a full-time human resources person or call center manager to focus on staffing. For smaller call centers, occasional staffing needs may be better handled by a service.

SELECTING THE RIGHT TECHNOLOGY

After you've staffed your call center and decided on its physical arrangement, it's time to add the driving tool that will make the whole mix work—the technology. In this book, I've talked about many different technologies, some of which may be relevant to your needs and some not. But, by now, you can probably see that choosing the right technology to round out your call center can be something of a challenge. That challenge is precisely my reason for writing this book.

Recently, while making sales calls in Scottsdale for my current employer, I walked into a call center that exemplified everything we've been discussing. This particular call center is the fulfillment end of a dot-com company, which was set up to help people relocate to and from cities all over the world.

It was all there—the prefab booths, the agents, the reader board on the wall, and the call queues and paths. There was even a spiral slide leading from the top floor to the lobby, where employees could get a quick thrill on their way out of the building. This tight, professional call center has accomplished its objectives by taking advantage of the best call center technologies available today.

My sincere hope is that this book will lead you to invest in the technologies that can most benefit *your* company's call center, thereby bringing it to the level of the call center I've just described. Doing so will help your business to evolve into a lean, efficient operation that enjoys improved business relationships and, ultimately, increased profits. That is my wish for you, and that is the goal of this book.

Building business and performance goals

To decide which technologies are right for your specific call center, you must first sit down and determine the goals and procedures that will provide the optimum experience for your customers, your agents, and your company. The technology you employ will be the foundation upon which these goals are built.

Write out exactly what your customer's experience should be when calling your call center. Set realistic goals for how you want your business to appear to callers. Do you want a human being to answer the phone within four rings every time? Do you want 24-hour coverage? Would you like callers to receive a message with a menu of choices for automated self-help? Will you cap your call queue at no longer than four minutes? Consider every possible detail of the entire interaction, and then map out the ideal experience.

What kind of goals will you have for your agents? Will there be sales quotas or call quotas? Decide whether you will use some type of customer service percentage measurement or a compound performance goal, such as a certain ratio of calls to sales made.

What tools does your management team expect to have in order to run the call center? Figure out how monitoring and reporting elements should be handled, and decide which cost and billing reports are needed. Is it important for your supervisors to be able to automatically input lists of prospect or customer telephone numbers for agents to dial?

Once you have a complete understanding of which technologies are available and how they can be applied to your business, your perceived needs will likely change. That's only natural. Imagine being isolated in the Amazon jungle for the past 15 years, completely out of touch with civilization. Wouldn't you be astounded by what a basic PC can do nowadays?

The mere existence of this wonderful machine drives many of our most important business decisions, but call center technology is no less important than a PC. Especially for those businesses that are highly dependent on telephone and electronic communications, purchasing the right call center technology becomes critical.

Chapter

11

A Primer on Purchasing

SELLING TELEPHONE AND CALL CENTER equipment has been a major part of my working life. I am proud of my involvement with the opportunities that have opened up for me. I have been a successful salesperson, but I want to be clear on one point.

Success in sales does not always mean achieving the absolute highest dollar volume, although I have held that honor a few times. It does not necessarily mean moving more voice mail systems than the next guy. To me, success in sales means doing the right thing for more customers than anyone else, thus earning your living with integrity and a clear conscience.

I think most salespeople in the world of telecommunications view success this way. We are more interested in finding a good opportunity to serve a customer with a real need, who also has the authority to make a purchase decision and the budget to justify the expenditure.

Such opportunities are much more satisfying than lining up gullible buyers for the latest gadget. Real satisfaction comes when we get to focus on the challenging—and fun—part of our job: developing creative solutions to business problems, or enhancing a company's success through our specialized knowledge of modern telecommunications systems.

To prepare you for the telecom marketplace, I'd like to take you on a guided tour of my side of the telecom world. It's the world of telecommunications systems and the people who sell them. I'd like to show you how the supply side of the customer/supplier equation works.

Buying telecom systems can be a complex exercise. You can't just run out to Office Depot and pull a predictive dialer off the shelf. It's not a simple retail purchase, so you must rely on a certain breed of company—the telephone system vendor.

The sale of a telephone system doesn't stop with purchasing equipment. Your system must be installed, programmed, and set up to meet your needs. And what about changes down the line, when you need more phones on your Panasonic digital phone system, or you decide to utilize a new software feature on your dialer? What do you do when you need to design and implement a new call flow in your interactive voice response server? You'll need help from those who know what they're doing—namely, the company that sold you your system.

WHERE TO BUY THE SYSTEM

There are three standard business models that sell, install, and service telecommunications equipment, including call center technologies. They are the actual manufacturers of the equipment, so-called trunkers, and interconnects or dealer/distributors.

Manufacturer direct

When you buy your telecommunications equipment manufacturer direct, you are usually dealing with the local or regional branch office of a large, even global, manufacturer. A good example is Lucent, the well-known manufacturer of business telephone systems, which also sells, installs, and services its products. (By the way, in the year 2000, Lucent reorganized itself into three different companies—Lucent, Avaya, and Expanets.) The main advantage of this distribution model is that you are dealing with the source of the equipment. Presumably, a manufacturer will know more about its systems than any other company.

Generally, a company this large also has the resources to pump tons of dollars into research and development for both new and existing products. If you buy its latest and greatest system, chances are good that it will be state of the art and that the company will be around long into the future. However, with the ever-increasing pace of mergers and acquisitions going on in business today, you may find yourself dealing with a different parent company or perhaps the same company under a different name.

You would think that buying directly from the manufacturer would yield the lowest price, but that's not always the case. In fact, the prices charged by manufacturer-distributors are often higher than other alternatives. Nonetheless, because these companies have deep pockets, I have seen them sell a system at far below cost simply to thwart a competitor.

The manufacturer-distributor model seems to work well for large, multinational or national companies. Their many branch offices provide a consistency across the enterprise that permits easier management and support for the company's customers. The downside of these companies, though, is also due to their size. For example, because their service departments are merely branch offices of a national corporate structure, price tags tend to be higher than what local companies charge. Naturally, when such a company is the only outlet for service or add-on equipment to its product, it doesn't have to worry about true competition in the marketplace. Therefore, it can set its pricing based on what the market will bear.

Then, there are the issues of control and flexibility. When purchasing something as critically important to your business as telecommunications equipment, there are often circumstances where you may feel you need to "go to the top" to get them resolved. Local managers of a large company do not always have the authority to make decisions on billing disputes or authorize overtime to fix technical failures. When trying to meet a scheduled installation deadline, these limitations can turn into a real problem.

Trunkers

At the other end of the distribution hierarchy are the suppliers I affectionately call "trunkers." Often, you'll find that a trunker used to work as some sort of technician for the phone company, but subsequently left and set up a small, one- or two-person operation. These entrepreneurs sell and install small telephone systems in addition to installing jacks, running computer or telephone wire, and servicing the older systems of their former employer.

New products sold by trunkers are typically phone systems that can be purchased at the local electrical supply house. Panasonic and Vodavi are two manufacturers that make such a basic phone system. Regardless of whether an individual has any knowledge or experience in telecom, he is within his rights to buy these systems over the counter and resell them to customers.

Not surprisingly, trunkers are also the most active outlet for the resale market. They locate old systems through private sales or used-system dealers and then turn them over for a profit. The bottom line is that trunkers are generally competent and knowledgeable former technicians, and, for simple installations, they may be your cheapest option.

Due to the small size of these outfits, you may have trouble getting hold of them if you are not their only customer. But, if you *are* the trunker's only customer, watch out. To help him make his mortgage payment this month, you could easily find yourself with many more system options than you need.

In my opinion, though, the most important disadvantage to buying from trunkers is that they do not have to be certified by a manufacturer to sell its product. Because they have not contracted to be a dealer for a specific manufacturer, they will have no manufacturer training under their belts, no special access to technical support, and you could be left without any recourse to manufacturer warranties on your purchase.

Dealer distributor: The interconnect

The happy medium is to buy from a locally or regionally based "interconnect" company. This generic name arises from the basic function of these companies, which is to interconnect business phone systems to the public telephone network.

Interconnects do not manufacture the equipment they sell and install, and they are generally dealers for more than one telephone system manufacturer. This fact works to the advantage of an interconnect's customers because the company will be able to offer different solutions to fit different circumstances.

Mitel SX-2000 Phone System

Courtesy of Mitel Corporation (www.mitel.com)

Most of the profit from selling and servicing telecommunications systems is derived from servicing the systems. A interconnect owner may take 10 percent of an expensive phone system sale to the bank, but his real profit comes from the long-term relationships he develops with his business customers. For these customers, a crew of technicians working at $50 to $100 per billing hour are hired out to provide all essential business services and add or replace hardware as needed.

Local ownership is a big advantage offered by interconnects. Should there be a problem with the sale, installation, or support of your purchase, the ultimate authority in the company is locally available. You'll be able to talk to him or her and resolve the issue immediately.

Most times, manufacturers that distribute through interconnects are smaller and more responsive than their big manufacturer-distributor competitors. This is advantageous to both the interconnects and their customers, because such manufacturers are pressured to please their dealers in order to stay competitive. Quite naturally, dealers are most happy when they have quality products and support to offer their customers, which, in turn, enables them to earn business and make money.

Often, a manufacturer will sign up with multiple dealers in a given geographical market. This situation means that if you are dissatisfied with the service you receive after you make your purchase, you have the option of switching to a different interconnect.

Manufacturers usually limit the number of competing interconnects they sign with, though. In this way, dealers have some degree of exclusivity in their regions, and manufacturers can keep their products in the hands of the most qualified interconnects.

To be accepted as a manufacturer's dealer, the interconnect will have to show a certain minimum sales volume predetermined by the manufacturer. Then, there is often a minimum annual volume that must be met just to stay qualified as a dealer. However, an interconnect can usually earn deeper discounting on the manufacturer's products if it sells at even higher volume levels.

There are some risks to doing business with an interconnect. These are usually small, local companies, so if they fail or otherwise close down, you will lose any long-term warranty given to you. Some dealers are now addressing this problem by awarding warranties that are underwritten by third-party insurance carriers, while other warranties are designed to convert to a new dealer if the original dealer goes out of business.

Because interconnects handle multiple products, you also run the risk that its technical staff will not be absolute experts on every system they sell, including the one you bought. Understandably, manufacturers that distribute their own products can offer you superior expertise. After a few years, the guy who does nothing but service Toshiba telephone systems is going to see every conceivable problem that can occur with a Toshiba system. Servicing provided by manufacturers tends to cost less because their technicians can diagnose and repair problems in very short order. Many dealers change products too frequently for their technicians to become expert on each one.

An interconnect is also more likely to hire journeymen technical staff who are new to telecom. These technicians generally receive only on-the-job training. In contrast, national companies have the resources to provide formal certification and training programs for new hires. Let me say, though, that on-the-job experience is not always a bad thing. Some of the worst-looking

installations I've ever seen were the product of 20-year telephone company techs who couldn't care less about the quality
of their work.

Finally, I want to tell you that there is an important exception
to the traditional, one-company, locally owned interconnect.
Sometimes, a company that may have begun as a locally owned
interconnect adds locations and gradually grows to become a
network of dealers across the country. Such companies are structured just like other interconnects and continue to serve as
manufacturer dealer-distributors, only on a national level. There
is an advantage to dealing with a larger, more established business, but the loss of local control in your area might be a disadvantage. Unless the company's headquarters are located in your
city, you'll forfeit being able to go directly to the owner to solve
problems.

Buying Used

The used and refurbished market is another outlet for the purchase of telephone equipment. Refurbished is a loose term for
equipment that has been remanufactured and returned to like-
new standards. In my experience, refurbished means something
more along the lines of "cleaned, painted, tested, and still working."

Businesses get rid of phone systems for many reasons. Maybe
there was a bankruptcy and the business was forced to liquidate
its assets. Or, perhaps, it's too expensive to relocate the phone
system to a new location. Oftentimes, a phone system is simply
outgrown. Also, a business at the end of a five-year lease may
decide it wants to upgrade rather than buying out the lease and
keeping what it has. Regardless of the reason, when phone systems are no longer needed, they frequently become available to
other businesses via the used and refurbished market.

Because of the rapid pace of technology, a phone system just five to eight years old may be all but obsolete. Today's hot new technology is tomorrow's doorstop. But, if your needs are simple, and you are able to clearly define what you want, buying a used system may not be a bad idea. Just be aware that there are four issues associated with this option that can become big headaches.

- **Installation and service**
  Remember, the system still has to be hung on the wall and configured to work for you. Unless you plan to do it yourself, add the cost of installation to the cost of your equipment. If not, you'll need to find someone qualified to install the system who also has access to technical documentation for the system. This last point is often a real problem, because documentation rarely comes with used equipment. The original dealers usually keep the technical docs in their offices, and most customers don't request a copy. Even if they did, it's likely been lost long ago.

- **Warranty**
  What warranty? A private individual or a business won't stand behind the product they've sold you, nor can they be expected to. Most used-system dealers extend to you a 90-day warranty on the equipment alone. Only rarely have I seen a full one-year warranty on a used system.

- **Parts**
  Telecommunications system manufacturers are constantly looking for ways to remain competitive, which means they are always developing technology for the future. Because most of their resources are devoted to new systems, there is a finite number of years during which

they will make parts for older models. Fifteen years is the max for some manufacturers, while others taper off after only five to seven years. Therefore, parts for an older system are often hard to come by.

- **Future innovation**
  Once a system has been deemed obsolete, its capability has effectively been frozen in time. I once owned a 1972 Ford Maverick. It was bright orange, and I loved it. But, it could never be equipped with an air bag, ABS brakes, or computerized fuel injection. Old phone systems are the same—they're difficult to upgrade.

YOUR THREE RELATIONSHIPS WITH YOUR VENDOR

When investigating the purchase of a call center solution, there are three different relationships you'll become involved in with your vendor. Each of the three relationships is vital for different reasons, and all are necessary for you to choose the supplier capable of delivering a system compatible with your business and its goals.

First, you have a relationship with the salesperson. Needless to say, you must be confident that your salesperson is fully knowledgeable about the products he's selling and experienced with the type of technology you're considering. Otherwise, how can he propose solutions for your specific business needs?

Salespeople only lead the charge, however, no matter how good they are. Unless they also own the business, they are merely representatives for the company that will be serving this critical component of your business. I suggest you interview salespeople as you would a prospective employee. Determine their history and their experience by asking for personal sales references. Most important are the recommendations of satisfied clients.

Second, you will have relationship with your vendor's installation crew. These people are responsible for installing, programing, and customizing your system. They are also the folks who will train your employees to use the new system. Besides knowing who these people are, you need to feel comfortable with the crew's competency, experience, and ability to look at things from the perspective of your business. Can you get references from other businesses that own similar systems installed by these same people? Can you meet the training personnel before you commit to your purchase?

Finally, you will have an ongoing relationship with your vendor's service department. Most interconnects use different employees to perform day-to-day service calls and routine maintenance than those used to install and set up new systems. Generally speaking, the crew that installs your phone system will not be the same people who come out to repair a dead phone 18 months after installation.

It is also important for you to know how your vendor handles routine service calls and add-on work. To keep their dealers honest, many manufacturers send independent surveys directly to customers, asking them to rate the dealers' overall performance. Is there a customer satisfaction report available on the dealer you are considering? How about reference letters? Can you speak with some of their established customers? Ask to preview the service agreement. You'll especially want to know your vendor's policies on response times, plus the labor billing rates for both regular and overtime service.

THE SALESPERSON'S JOB

Later section of this chapter, I'll outline how these three vendor relationships—salesperson, installation crew, and service department—impact the entire purchase process. Together, they form the framework for purchasing telecom equipment. But, first, allow me to show you a glimpse of the world of the telecom salesperson. If you have ever been in any other kind of sales position, I'm sure it will seem quite familiar to you.

Prospecting

As a salesperson, I had three main jobs to accomplish on any given day. Along with assorted related duties, my main job was to find new opportunities to sell telecommunications equipment. Sometimes, these opportunities came to me in the form of referrals.

Perhaps a satisfied customer told a colleague about me or my company. Or, maybe the woman I bought my house from told her brother to call me about a phone system for his new business. At other times, existing customers wanting to upgrade or expand their current systems called for help.

I might also get leads from newspaper articles announcing the expansion plans of area businesses. Or, sometimes I would call on an old contact in a company I knew was relocating to see if I could help plan its move (from the perspective of its telecommunications systems). Most of the time, however, new opportunities came from cold-calling—walking into a business I'd never visited before and asking to speak with the person responsible for telephone equipment.

Those were fishing trips, of course, and I knew that 95 percent of the businesses I approached were not going to be interested in a proposal from me. But, my job wasn't to make this 95 percent buy something they didn't need. My job was to find the remaining 5 percent that might be receptive to what I had to offer. These businesses included those interested in upgrading their telecommunications equipment, as well as those outgrowing an old system, moving to new offices, or starting a call center.

Qualification

Once I had a genuine prospect, I then had to figure out what the likelihood of turning the opportunity into an actual sale might be. Who has time to spend on a prospect if there's no chance of converting it to a sale? This can happen all too frequently. For example, some people like to use a competitor's salesperson just to get a better price from their existing vendor. They have no intention of buying from the salesperson; they simply want to keep their vendor honest. Would you want to spend hours designing a system for an employee who has no authority to buy or for a boss who has no interest in what you have to offer?

The process of qualification requires delicacy and diplomacy. As tactfully as possible, salespeople need to determine if the prospect has a need for the product, is qualified to make the final purchase decision, and has the money to buy the it. Without qualifying a prospect, the salesperson can spend a lot of time selling ice to Eskimos, so to speak, at the expense of pursuing solid leads that will eventually pay off.

Qualification also means determining the exact needs of the customer. A good salesperson asks a lot of questions about what the prospect wants to accomplish, such as: What are the goals of the call center? How is the caller's experience envisioned? What kind of management reporting will be required? A good salesperson does a lot of listening at a qualification, or needs analysis, meeting. Poor salespeople tend to do all the talking, going on and on about what they, their company, and the equipment can do.

Presentation

If your salesperson possesses a deep understanding of the technology and product line he represents, and if he has listened well to your needs, you should receive a proposal for exactly the kind of system you should consider buying. If you asked for predictive dialing and get a proposal for IVR, your salesperson did not understand your requirements.

Often you can preview a working model of the system you are considering in specially equipped rooms at the interconnect's offices. In other situations, the vendor may take you to an existing customer's site. For simple sales, your salesperson may present a PowerPoint slide show or a written proposal.

If at all possible, I think seeing the actual system is a much better way to understand what's being proposed. You will get a visceral understanding of the technology, and, at the same time, you can see whether the salesperson is comfortable with what is being proposed. In my opinion, confidence is a big selling point. The salesperson who looks me squarely in the eye and tells me that this is the absolute right product for my company's needs inspires me to take his advice.

Though a good presentation is often vital to making a successful sale, some salespeople overemphasize the process and spend too much time and energy on this one activity. If the prospect's entire relationship with a salesperson consists of their interactions in a presentation meeting, then many important steps are missed on the way to making a wise and informed decision.

Overcoming objections

As a prospective buyer, you have given your salesperson all the information he needs to design a solution for you. The design has been gone over by the vendor's engineers and technical staff to be sure it is exactly the right thing for your business. Now it's time for yes or no, but you're not quite ready to commit.

Maybe you want to look at one more competitor's package. Perhaps the price is higher than your budget allows, or you're not sure you need one element of the overall proposal. It may be that your partner needs to look it over with you. Then again, maybe you don't think the warranty is long enough. Perhaps you're concerned about a negative reference from one of the vendor's customers, or you're concerned that the vendor has been in business for only two years.

Experienced salespeople have heard them all, but a good salesperson will be attuned to your reasons for not committing to the proposal right now. To move the sale forward, your salesperson must be able to address each objection and resolve it to your satisfaction. Often, there are reasonable answers to almost every question. Sometimes, though, the answers you get will not be enough to overcome your objections, so the sale ends up going to a competitor.

I never begrudge customers for going with another vendor. I know that I have done my job properly and have presented the best phone system I can offer. If a customer finds something lacking that can be provided by another vendor, who can fault him? Salespeople know they cannot make every sale.

Closing

"Closing" is such an overused word. In sales talk, closing has traditionally meant the point at which you wrestle a "yes" out of your customer after he's told you "no" 20 times. Some over-zealous, misguided salespeople feel compelled to pull out their 500-page sales manual on closing techniques and keep trying until the prospect throws them off the property.

Nowadays, most salespeople consider this antiquated approach to be unprofessional. If customers are not ready to say yes, most likely it is because they have unanswered questions, legitimate objections, or there is a point they don't fully understand. In these cases, "no" really means no. It is certainly not the time for the salesperson to try the Ben Franklin close, who is said to have made major decisions by listing all the pros and cons first.

From initial contact through closing, the selling process should have moved steadily forward with definable milestones between each stage. If the rest of the sale has been conducted professionally, the closing is then nothing more than the natural conclusion of things. A purchase agreement is signed, the installation date is set, and the client writes a deposit check. That's it.

Now, however, let's put ourselves on the other side of the desk and view things from the perspective of the purchaser. What course of action will give the purchaser some control of the situation? That's the topic of the next section, where I'll show you how to qualify the proposals of different vendors. Finally, I'll wrap up this chapter with a checklist of 10 tips that can help you maximize your buying experience and purchase the best call center technology for your company.

THE PURCHASING PROCESS

Purchasing telecommunications equipment actually mirrors the selling process. Being able to identify where you are during the purchasing process enables you to control the sale and end up with exactly what you want.

To start, write out in plain English precisely what you expect to accomplish with your purchase. Do you have a clear vision of the system you want to buy? Do you know that your company needs a predictive dialer, or do you need a voice mail system with an automated attendant feature?

The answers are not always so clear, however, so it is a good idea to write a description of what you want your caller's experience to be. Then write down what your agent's experience should be, plus which management tools you'd like to have in your system. The more explicit your description is, the more power you have when selecting a vendor.

If possible, find a company similar to yours with a telecommunications system that includes many of the features you want. Then, use this system as a model to build your own application. Though you may own stock in Lucent Technologies and favor steering your spending that way, I recommend you avoid locking yourself up with a specific brand name or manufacturer. As much as possible, you want to be open to the options the market has to offer.

Also, unless you are absolutely sure you have narrowed your need down to a particular technology, it pays to keep an open mind. For example, if you are looking for ways to increase the number of lines into your office for long-distance calls, bidding for a channel bank and T1 service from a long-distance carrier may appear to be the right thing to do. But, you could be closing the door on other alternatives that are available from your vendor. In short, being too specific limits your possibilities. Focus on the application and what you want to achieve, but be amenable to alternatives and suggestions.

Prospecting

As I've described earlier, salespeople go fishing for prospective customers who may be ripe to purchase what they're selling. In the same fashion, buyers should assemble a pool of potential vendors ready to develop proposed solutions for their needs. By contacting a range of vendors, you can be assured of seeing what the market has to offer at the most competitive prices. Don't call any more than five or ten, though. Eventually, you'll have to narrow your choice to three or four possibilities.

If you're happy with your current vendor, by all means, start there. Let your regular salesperson know that you are going to solicit a few competitive proposals as well. Do you remember my suggestion about finding a business similar to your own with a phone system you think you might like? If you have based your planning on such a model system, be sure to call the vendor responsible for that system.

Then, investigate the open market by using referrals from friends or even the yellow pages (as a last resort). It's a good idea to choose a mix of large and small companies, including national chains and local enterprises. If some of the PC- and router-based phone systems described earlier in this book sound intriguing to you, you'll want to put a data VAR (value-added reseller) in the mix.

Qualification and needs analysis

Next, interview candidate salespeople just as you would prospective new employees. Ask for their "resume" of experience, keeping in mind that many years of experience is not always equivalent to a deep understanding today's technology. See if you can learn a little about the company, such as how long they've been in business. How many customers do they serve? How extensive is their product line?

A very good qualifying question is to ask about the ratio of salespeople to technicians. A well-balanced company may have as many as three to five technicians for every salesperson, which indicates a solid base of business in your market. It also signifies that the company has developed good relationships with many customers, meaning its business is supported through servicing telephone systems and not solely through new equipment sales.

A prospective vendor's main mission should be to acquire your company as a new service customer through the sale of equipment. Its objective should never be limited to making a few dollars on the sale itself. Telecommunications equipment needs to be frequently maintained, periodically reprogrammed, and occasionally upgraded. Those companies employing only one or two technicians for every salesperson are too focused on new sales to provide good service over the long term.

That said, you'll want to meet the first round of eligible candidates, either individually or as a group. Inform them that this is an exploratory session only. During the meeting, answer their questions honestly and share your history with your current vendor, revealing both what you like and don't like about the service you have.

Then, outline what you're looking for and ask for preliminary opinions. In response, you should hear proposals for the technologies you expect to employ. For example, if you describe something that involves call queuing and a supervisor station that can monitor calls, the salesperson should be talking to you about an ACD system.

Pay close attention to the salespeople who ask good questions and who seem to have a good grasp of the technology. Do they appear confident in their ability to provide you with the solutions you want? Lastly, invite the top four candidates to return at a later time and present their solutions.

Presentation

You may be able to see a presentation of the system you are considering at the vendor's facility. If so, that's the perfect time to introduce yourself to the technical staff, check out the scope of the operation, and meet its owner or top manager.

The presentation is also the time for you to ask those questions that you will need answered before you're sure this is the right system for your company. Be sure to include the following questions:

- Is the price within your budget or way off the mark?

- Does the price include everything on the proposal, or will you incur additional costs before the system is completely operational?

- Do you know exactly which features come with the system?

- Which features will you have to purchase later if you decide to expand the system?

- What are the upper capacity limits of the system?

- What space and environmental resources—electrical power, air conditioning, or backboard space—are you required to provide?

- Would you be comfortable committing to a long-term business relationship with this vendor?

After each presentation, even the last one, tell your salesperson you will contact him as soon as you review your remaining proposals. Never make a commitment during the presentation.

Overcoming objections

It's now time to narrow your vendor candidates down to two. Consider any unresolved issues from your presentation meetings with these two vendors. Ask each about attractive features and services offered by other vendors to see if these finalists can include them as well. Are there any sales promotions being run by the manufacturer that would reduce the cost of your system?

Then ask to visit the person who will be installing the system, the training personnel, and the owner or top manager. You'll want to meet the whole team, so that you can feel comfortable with all aspects of your new relationship with this vendor. If possible, you'll also want to see a working system at another customer's site.

Finally, when you have made two solid choices, tell both that you are considering a competitive offer and ask them for their absolute best prices and packages. Even though your first choice may already be cheaper, this tactic usually gains some kind of concession for you, such as an extra $1,000 off the price tag or an extra year's warranty. It never hurts to ask.

Close

Now that you have made a final choice, I'd like to request a personal favor. I believe that selling telecommunications systems and services successfully requires a special kind of salesperson. I estimate that only 20 percent of the salespeople in the telecom industry belong to this special group. Here's why.

To design the best technological solution for your particular business, your salesperson had to listen very carefully to you. Then, he or she helped you to justify the expense to your company while fighting for the best possible price and terms from her company. In short, your salesperson put your needs before his at every step—so, please reward him for the effort. You could take him to lunch to sign the paperwork, or send a thank you letter to her boss. Best of all, refer him to someone else who may need a new system.

Remember that this one salesperson has made a huge impact on one of the most important aspects of your business. In addition, he or she can continue to serve as a great ongoing resource for your business. With that in mind, it certainly makes sense to show your appreciation.

At the closing, go through all the paperwork carefully. If you are not fully satisfied, ask to have everything explained until you are. Be sure to confirm the following: the stated price and what is included, the terms of your warranty, and the timeline for your installation. Verify that you and your vendor have agreed on a follow-up schedule for any post-installation work, such as routine maintenance, prescheduled upgrades, training sessions, and so on. Also, confirm the scope of your responsibilities during the installation.

10 DETAILS—Take care of them *before* you sign the paperwork!

The following checklist summarizes some of the points we have discussed and introduces a few new ones. You'll want to consult this list at the conclusion of your purchase. Doing so may help you avoid many of the miscommunications and hidden expenses that can accompany the sale and installation of complex call center technology.

1. Itemized price breakdown

Most telecommunications and call center systems are built by assembling components within a contained system. For example, a voice mail system may feature anywhere from four ports to sixteen ports depending on the number of port cards installed with the system. When you understand what the elemental parts of the system are and know the price of each part, you can make better decisions about the final proposed sale.

Purchasing your call center system should be handled much the same way you would purchase a new car. Think of the itemized lists you see plastered on the windows of new cars, where the individual cost of each available option is broken out. If the five-CD disc changer and the moon roof are going to put you over your $20,000 budget, you simply strip them out of the package or try to get them thrown in at no extra charge. You can do the same with your phone system package.

2. Pre- and post-cut pricing

The "cut" is interconnect lingo for the cut-over date, which is when the new system becomes operational. The price of individual system elements, such as line cards or telephone sets, is usually different before and after the installation date. The cost for components and add-ons are higher when they are purchased separately after the installation, because they are not part of the original package.

Ask your vendor what the cost of individual components will be if you add them to the total package before the installation is complete. Then, compare that figure to the cost of adding them afterwards. When asking about post-cut pricing, ask also for a time guarantee. For example, if a telephone for your PBX/ACD system costs $225 pre-cut and $292 post-cut, can the post-cut price be guaranteed for one year from the installation date?

3. Turnkey price

When you and your vendor agree on the total, bottom-line price, be sure that it is a turnkey price. The total amount you are asked to pay for the system should include installation and a fully operational system that performs in accordance with its documentation. If you are purchasing an IVR system, for example, the price should include everything that is needed to make it perform as intended—installation, programming, setup, training, plus miscellaneous costs (wires, connectors, jacks, and so on).

4. Holdout percentage

On 75 percent of the equipment installations I have been part of, there are usually one or two nagging details left after the install is over. Sometimes it's a training class that needs to be scheduled, or one phone that doesn't work, or one IVR path that has not been programmed into the system. To ensure that such final issues get resolved, see if you can hold back a small percentage of the sale from final payment, say 10 percent. Both parties must agree to this arrangement, however, or you'll be considered delinquent in your payment.

If you lease or finance your system, do not sign the final delivery and acceptance papers until all issues are resolved. These legal documents tell the lease companies to release payment to the vendor, after which they begin billing you for your monthly payments.

5. Extended warranty

Most manufacturers of telecommunications equipment offer a one year warranty through their dealers. To gain a competitive advantage in their markets, many dealers will extend the warranty to two years. Some vendors have also formed underwriting cooperatives, effectively purchasing a form of insurance on new systems. Approximately 5 percent of the total cost of a new system is placed into a collective escrow account, which is then used to reimburse warranty claims to any member of the group. Under this arrangement, warranties may last up to five years.

Your should expect to receive the longest warranty being offered by the various competing vendors, but you can then ask your vendor to consider extending it by another year. This is a low-cost concession for a vendor to make.

6. Live demo

Either visit a company that has installed a system similar to the one you are considering, or have your vendor give you a live demonstration on a working version of the system. Demos may be run at the manufacturer's plant, the vendor's facility, or at your office. Just insist that you see a demonstration before you buy.

7. Guaranteed installation timeline

Ask your vendor to set up a firm timetable for the installation. It should cover all the steps necessary to complete the system, including training classes, technical meetings, and on-site technical time. It should also indicate when customer responsibilities need to be met. This timeline is used to manage the cut over, so it's very important that it is realistic and complete. Setting a timeline with your vendor also avoids unnecessary confusion about who was supposed to do what or when.

8. Meet the installer

It's always a good idea to meet the people who will perform the actual installation, preferably in an informal setting. Having a good working relationship with the installer or the project manager can go a long way towards ensuring that the cut goes smoothly. You get to see whether you're comfortable with the company's resources, and, hopefully, you will begin to establish a positive working relationship with these key people. Much of the common miscommunication that occurs on system installations can be avoided if the principal players—you and the installer—are working together on the same page.

9. Meet the service dispatcher

Bring some donuts into the vendor's office one Monday morning, and introduce yourself to the service dispatcher. This is the person who will send the technicians out to fix any bugs that crop up in your system. All day long he fields calls from disgruntled customers—all he hears about are problems. But, if you are more than just another voice on the phone to him, you may get better treatment. So, introduce yourself in person, say hello, and treat him with respect. When you need repair service, he'll know who you are.

10. Free coordination with carriers

Changing needs in your call center operation sometimes require changes with your local or long-distance telephone service. These issues can be frustrating time-wasters for you, so insist that your vendor be the one to communicate service changes to your carriers.

Vendors deal with the carriers every day, and they know how to make the proper requests for changes to service. Because they and the carriers speak the same language, changes for the cut over are made more smoothly and any potential miscommunication can be avoided. Though it then becomes the vendor's job to correct any problems that come up, most have no problem committing to that responsibility.

12

Managing a
Successful Cut Over

I INTRODUCED THE TERM "cut over" earlier in this book. It refers to the moment when the old way of doing things ends and the new system is fired up and put in use for the first time. In fact, "cut over" literally means cutting the telephone lines from the old system and moving them over to the new system.

The final installation of telecommunications equipment of any type also takes place during the cut over. This is the last step in the new system's installation, which occurs only after the system has been mounted and powered up, the programming has been keyed in, and the phones have been unpacked and set out on everyone's desk. To avoid disrupting business as usual, cut overs are usually scheduled for either overnight or a Friday.

In the telephone system world, including the call center world, small cut overs can be completed during a normal business day. More complicated installations take more time, naturally, and they are best done if the whole operation can be temporarily shut down.

The goal of any interconnect vendor is to prepare and plan for a new system's installation so well that the cut over becomes a mere formality. Most of these vendors understand that business cannot come to a complete stop just to install equipment. In addition, there are things your company can do on its end to ensure that the cut over runs as smoothly as possible.

DO YOUR PART

Make sure all tasks for which your company is responsible are completed on time. For example, if you're supposed to have an extra electrical outlet installed for the new system, be sure it gets done early. If you're supposed to come up with a call flow diagram for the IVR system, finish it.

Likewise, if the vendor needs an employee list to program your agent log-in software, provide it sooner than expected. In this way, you can set the tone of how the project will be handled, and you will avoid problems later on. Installing technicians are always busy and frequently overtaxed by their employers. You'll earn their appreciation if you're the customer who's easy to work with and helpfully involved in the process.

KEEP THE TIMELINE

It's perfectly okay to stay in touch with the installers on how they're progressing with the installation. You've already established a timeline with the vendor, right? The timeline includes a checklist of items that need to be accomplished with the approximate date for the completion of each task.

In a diplomatic way, of course, stay on top of the timeline with your installers. If things are sliding, ask if there's any way you can help get them back on track. There are many reasons why projects may fall behind. Some are avoidable—miscommunication or poor scheduling—while others are not, such as waiting for parts that haven't been delivered to the vendor. You'll want to know about these things as they happen rather than being surprised on the day you expect your system to be up and running.

BE SERIOUS ABOUT TRAINING

It is usually the vendor's responsibility to train your staff on how to operate the new system. Actually, it should be part of your company's contract. However, I have found that many vendors are somewhat slipshod in this regard.

It is vital that your staff receive some end-user training before the system installation is completed. How can you take full advantage of your new investment if your people are just begin to learn it on the day it is cut over? Imagine the chaos as your staff drops calls, upsets customers, and generally loses business for you. You can avoid all such unpleasantness by seeing that your agents are well-trained ahead of time. In fact, it is a good idea for everyone in your company to attend the training sessions even if they're not actively involved in the call center.

Being serious about training also means learning from the installers. Watch what they are doing and talk to them about the work they are doing. With support documentation, maybe some of the programming is simple enough that you can perform basic tasks in-house. For example, setting up new employees on your ACD system without calling the vendor can save you $100 or more in service charges.

Being able to tweak the call flow programming in-house can also help you keep the vendor's expensive technician away. And wouldn't it be great to build your own voice mail trees? Or wire in a new module for your monitoring system? Or build and load your own predictive dialer lists? Or reroute a DID extension so that calls to an employee who has left the company can ring to someone else's desk?

KNOW WHEN TO CRY WOLF

I call this tactic "strategic whining," and, in all modesty, I must say that I am somewhat of a master at this technique. Vendors do their best to schedule their resources, but, whether real or perceived, emergencies often sidetrack them. Therefore, you need to know how to bring attention to yourself without abusing your relationship with the vendor. Sometimes it's necessary to bypass the person you're dealing with and state your case to his superior, but to do so dramatically is an art.

You must never use anger or intimidation, but neither should you allow your business to be taken for granted. It must be earned. If your installation timeline is slipping unreasonably, or if your training class has been cancelled without being re-scheduled, or if you receive an invoice for work that was part of the installation, don't hesitate to run your concern up the chain of command.

Be reasonable, but unrelenting. Tell the person you speak to: "I expected it to happen this way, and no one has told me anything is different. So, your people need to be here today." Be angry in a calm way. Express your disappointment, pointing out that you have taken great pains to choose the right vendor and prepare the groundwork for the installation. Hold your vendor to the proposal you both agreed to.

TELL YOUR CUSTOMERS

Have you ever called a place of business, asked to speak to someone, and heard the following? "I'm going to try and transfer you, but if we're disconnected, call back at the following number," or, "We just installed a new system, so bear with me."

Your existing customers have called your business many times, so they have an established idea of how their calls are going to be handled. If their next experience varies significantly from that preconception, you have created a whole new impression with your customer. Such an impression may be good. But, if it's bad, chances are you'll never know because the customer won't call you again.

If your customers are going to affected by changes in your call center, I suggest you prepare them. You could send them a postcard that says you've invested in upgrades to serve them better, or you could send out a notice with your billing statements. Or, you may want to add a recorded notice to the first message in your ACD queue or the preamble on your automated attendant.

When telling your customers to expect a change in how their calls are handled, be sure to mention that the change was made with them in mind. Who's not going to be on your side with that explanation?

CELEBRATE

Think of how many people are affected by a major change in the technology that serves your business. If yours is a minor change, then only a few people might be affected. But if you're building or revamping a call center, you're impacting the day-to-day lives of all your employees, not to mention your customers. Then, there's the salesperson for the vendor and the entire vendor team, including technicians and trainers. They have been held to tight professional standards, and they have probably worked very hard to ensure a successful installation.

When it's all over and the work is complete, it's time to celebrate a job well done. Bring pizza in for everyone, or buy a six-pack of beer for the installers. A few dollars and some goodwill invested at this time will pay off when you need to have these people fix something down the road. Besides which, if all has gone well and the installation is flawless, you indeed have something to celebrate.

CLOSING WORDS

We've covered a wide range of topics in this book, from learning how a basic telephone line works to running through the options on a multimedia call center server. The world of telecommunications is full of complex technology, but I trust I was able to explain some of it in a way that was neither too complicated nor too simple.

For most business people, a telecommunications decision is just one more task in a pile of tasks that have to be dealt with. But, it is critically important for you to understand what today's call center technology can do for you. With the possible exception of computers, there is no other technology that will have a greater impact on your business.

If it is now time for you to build or improve your business call center, I wish you luck. Also, before you close the cover of this book and go off to other things, I want to thank you for investing your time in this work. I hope it has been helpful and will continue to be helpful in your future.

Again, I wish you luck in your endeavors and hope our paths cross again.

Appendix A

CALL CENTER ORGANIZATIONS

Like every other industry today, the designers, managers, and employees of the call center industry are well represented by trade organizations. Some groups publish online articles of interest to the call center community; some perform call center benchmark tests; and others provide networking and fellowship opportunities among people holding similar job titles. In addition, there are groups devoted to helping businesses locate manufacturers, consultants, and suppliers of call center technology.

Whether you want to develop new skills or add to your knowledge base, the organizations listed below offer ample resources for personal growth. Often, the focus of a particular organization is apparent by its name, but not always. Therefore, don't let a name deter you from investigating any group that sparks your interest.

American Teleservices Association

Suite 615
1620 I Street NW
Washington, DC 20006
202-293-2452
www.ataconnect.org

American Productivity and Quality Center
3rd Floor
123 North Post Oak Lane
Houston, TX 77024
713-681-4020
www.apqc.org

Call Centre Management Association
GPO Box 1552P
Melbourne, Victoria 3001
AUSTRALIA
011-61-1300-301-390
www.ccma.asn.au

Central Station Alarm Association
Suite 201
440 Maple Avenue East
Vienna, VA 22180
703-242-4670
www.csaaul.org

Customer Care Institute
17 Dean Overlook NW
Atlanta, GA 30318
404-352-9291
www.customercare.com

The Direct Marketing Association, Inc.
1120 Avenue of The Americas
New York, NY 10036-8700
212-790-1500
www.the-dma.org

Help Desk Institute
Suite 301
6385 Corporate Drive
Colorado Springs, CO 80919
800-248-5667
www.helpdeskinst.com

Incoming Calls Management Institute
P. O. Box 6177
Annapolis, MD 21401-0177
410-267-0700
www.incoming.com

International Customer Service Association
401 North Michigan Avenue
Chicago, IL 60611
800-360-4272
www.icsa.com

Society of Consumer Affairs Professionals in Business
Suite 404
801 North Fairfax Street
Alexandria, VA 22314
703-519-3700
www.socap.org

Appendix B

CALL CENTER PUBLICATIONS

While writing this book, I consulted a wide variety of industry publications. For those of you who want to learn more about call centers and the telecommunications field in general, I would recommend the following:

Art Sobczak's *TelE-sales*
13254 Stevens Street
Omaha, NE 68137
402-895-9399
www.businessbyphone.com

Call Center Magazine
CMP Media, Inc.
12 West 21st Street
New York, NY 10010
888-824-9793
www.callcentermagazine.com

C@ll Center CRM Solutions
Technology Marketing Corporation
One Technology Plaza
Norwalk, CT 06854
800-243-6002
www.tmcnet.com

CC News—The Business Newspaper for Contact Center and Customer Care Professionals
United Publications
P. O. Box 995
106 Lafayette Street
Yarmouth, ME 04096
207-846-0600
www.ccnews.com

Call Center News Service (*Call Center Savvy*)
Dawson Publishing
718-788-6220
www.callcenternews.com

Computer Telephony
CMP Media, Inc.
12 West 21st Street
New York, NY 10010
888-824-9793
www.computertelephony.com

Communications News
Nelson Publishing, Inc.
2500 Tamiami Trail North
Nokomis, FL 34275
941-966-9521
www.comnews.com

Customer Interface Magazine
Advanstar
Suite 600
201 Sandpointe Avenue
Santa Ana, CA 92707
714-513-8829
www.c-interface.com

Customer Support Management
Intertec Publishing, a Primedia Company
P. O. Box 4949
11 River Bend Drive South
Stamford, CT 06907-0949
203-358-9900
www.customersupportmgmt.com

Direct Magazine
Intertec Publishing, a Primedia Company
P. O. Box 4265
11 River Bend Drive South
Stamford, CT 06907-0265
203-358-9900
www.directmag.com

IT Support News
United Publications
106 Lafayette Street
Yarmouth, ME 04096
207-846-0600
www.ccnews.com

Operations & Fulfillment
Intertec Publishing, a Primedia Company
P. O. Box 4949
11 River Bend Drive South
Stamford, CT 06907-0949
www.opsandfulfillment.com

Teleconnect
CMP Media, Inc.
12 West 21st Street
New York, NY 10010
888-824-9793
www.teleconnect.com

Glossary

1FB (one flat-rate business) line
An industry term referring to the single telephone lines used to provide local telephone service to businesses. Other terms interchangeable with 1FB include CO (central office) line and POTS (plain old telephone service) line. The phone company charges a flat monthly rate for this service, hence the designation "flat" business line. All calls made within your local calling area are covered by 1FB service. Per-minute charges do not apply.

1MB (one metered business) line
This line delivers the same telephone service as a 1FB line, but local calls are charged a metered, per-minute rate.

A

AA
See automated attendant.

abandoned caller
This term refers to a caller who hangs up while waiting in an ACD queue. By reading the ANI (phone number) information of an incoming call, advanced call centers can track abandoned callers. Such tracking helps managers determine how long

customers will tolerate waiting in a queue. Sometimes, if enough phone numbers can be matched to clients in a center's database, the call centers might institute a callback policy for abandoned callers.

account codes

Many phone systems require an agent to enter a numeric code on his telephone keypad either during or immediately after a telephone call. Such codes categorize callers for entry into the phone system's reporting functions.

For example, a company that advertises in different magazines could assign a different account code for each magazine. Agents first ask callers where they learned about the company and then enter the appropriate account code based on their answers. When a report is later compiled, managers can determine which advertising was the most effective in generating leads.

ACD

See automatic call distributor.

automatic call distributor (ACD)

Whether a stand-alone system or a PBX function, automatic call distributors are used to answer incoming calls when all agents are busy. ACD is able to distribute calls evenly among available agents by using algorithms to balance work flow. This system can also play greetings, recorded messages, and hold music, thereby entertaining and informing callers while they wait.

ACD group

Special ACD programming sorts agents into groups according to the queues they are responsible for or by skill level (their ability to answer certain types of calls).

ACD log in

When agents report to work on a given shift, they must announce their availability to the ACD system by logging in. Logging in also tells the system which groups or skill levels agents are assigned to and enables management to track the activity of individual agents for reporting purposes.

ACD make busy

This ACD function allows agents to take themselves off the system's availability list without completely logging out. A "make busy" entry shows up in reporting differently than a log-out, so breaks and non-telephone work can be accounted for separately.

ACD path/ACD queue

An ACD path is a sequence of events within the system's programming that will determine what callers hear and where they will be routed as they wait for an available agent. Most ACD systems can be programmed with multiple paths so that different types of incoming calls can be handled in different ways.

ACD supervisor help key

This feature permits agents to access their shift supervisor whenever they feel such assistance is required. In some systems, pressing the help key will actually bring the supervisor right into the call. In others, a silent monitoring session will be established, but the supervisor retains the ability to enter into the call as well when necessary.

ACD reporting

ACDs have the ability to compile and store statistical information on the incoming calls that they handle. You can install a reporting package on your ACD system that will detail the activity of your call center in the areas you choose.

ACD unavailable
See ACD make busy.

ACD wrap-up timer
At the completion of a telephone call, call center agents usually have some sort of wrap-up work to do, such as paperwork, closing a customer's record, or entering call statistics. An ACD wrap-up timer lists an agent as temporarily unavailable for a predetermined interval (say, 30 to 90 seconds) after each completed call. Wrap-up times may be overridden by the agent on a call-by-call basis if desired.

agent
A call center employee responsible for handling the customer interactions of a given business, whether telephone calls, email, or fax transmissions.

agent desktop
In this book, this term refers to any computer software program that acts as an interface between an agent and any type of call center technology. For example, the agent desktop for a multimedia call center server is the multimedia queue window. For a predictive dialer, it is the terminal where an agent sees call information appear in conjunction with incoming telephone calls. For an ACD system with CTI capability, the agent desktop consists of the customer database software that pops up simultaneously with the arrival of a phone call.

analog (telephone signaling)
A signal that features a continuous nature rather than a pulsed or discrete nature. Electrical or physical analogies, such as continuously varying voltages, frequencies, or phases, may be used as analog signals. Voice signals, including telephone and radio, have traditionally been sent using analog transmissions.

Analog is actually a shortened form of "analogous," referring to the fact that when voice is transmitted over twisted pairs of copper wire, the electric signals will fluctuate (in volume and pitch) in the same pattern as the original signal.

ANI
See automatic number identification.

ATM
See asynchronous transfer mode.

automatic number identification (ANI)
This feature utilizes a method of transmission known as in-band signaling, which embeds additional information about any call directly into the call signal itself. In this way, your long-distance telephone carrier can pass along signals to your phone system that represent the phone numbers of your callers.

asynchronous transfer mode (ATM)
This packet-based data transmission protocol allows carriers to bond voice and data signals together into one digital carrier circuit.

automated attendant (AA)
Automated attendants are functions of your phone system that act as an automated receptionist. An AA can answer incoming telephone calls with a recorded greeting that asks callers choose from a menu: "1" for sales, "2" for administration, "3" for service, and so on. Some automated attendants allow callers to dial telephone extensions as well.

automatic dialer
See predictive dialer.

B

basic rate interface (BRI)

One of the two ISDN (integrated services digital networking) protocols. BRI partitions a copper telephone line into one carrier channel for signaling information plus two bearer channels (64 kbps each) to carry traffic. Traffic may be either voice or data, such as a connection to a corporate LAN or Internet service provider. Also, the bearer channels can be used separately for voice or data, or they can be bonded together to establish one high-speed data connection at 128 kbps.

C

call accounting system

This system may be either free-standing hardware or software added to an existing system. Its function is to capture call information (SMDR) from a business telephone system and store it for later retrieval as a report. For example, hotels use call accounting systems to track telephone calls made from guests' rooms in order to charge back the cost to the guests. Or businesses may use these systems to allocate telephone costs to various departments or employees.

call center

This term refers to any business, or unit within a business, that is established primarily for the purpose of communicating by telephone with customers, vendors, and suppliers.

call sequencer

By locating this device between incoming telephone lines and your telephone system, your business gains the ability to put incoming calls on hold until agents become available to answer them.

caller ID (identification)

Using in-band signaling, local telephone companies can transmit a caller's telephone number (ID) along with an incoming telephone call. However, your telephone or telephone system must be appropriately equipped to read, display, or otherwise make use of the information.

central office (CO) line

The basic, analog copper telephone line used to provide dial tone from your local phone company. *See* 1FB

channel bank

This device is installed at the customer's premises, where its job is to break up a T1 line (supplied by the phone company) into individual channels. The channels may then be connected to either individual telephones or a telephone system.

circular hunting

See also hunting. When all lines in a group are busy, the hunting process passes calls from one line to the next among a preprogrammed group of lines until an available line is found. In contrast, circular hunting "circles" from the last member of the group back to the first and continues around the group until the call is answered.

CLEC

See competitive local exchange carrier.

CO line

See central office line.

CO line card

In a business telephone system, this card is the circuit board that connects the system to the incoming CO lines.

competitive local exchange carrier (CLEC)

Due to the deregulation of local telephone service in 1996, the established local phone companies, known as incumbent local exchange carriers (ILECs), no longer have a monopoly in their business. Any company wishing to compete directly in the local phone service market may do so, hence the name competitive local exchange carrier (CLEC).

computer telephony integration (CTI)

This term refers to technology that joins together a computer processing system and a telephone system. The systems may be connected by both a physical link (usually a cable) and logical connections, such as software that allows one system to share information with and/or exercise control over the other.

A good example of this type of technology is the "screen pop" application. In this case, whenever the phone system receives an incoming call, it also picks up the caller's phone number (via ANI) and passes it along to the call center's customer database. The computer system then automatically accesses the customer's record and displays it on the screen of the agent receiving the call.

CRM

See customer relationship management.

customer assurance server

A server-based solution that permits agents' calls to be recorded and played back. The customer assurance server is more advanced than standard, hard-wired monitoring systems, may also be capable of making a live record of the activity on an agent's PC monitor simultaneously with the associated call.

customer relationship management (CRM)

Whether a free-standing system or a software program, CRM allows a business to track and manage its contacts and customer relationships. Most CRM systems can connect customer database information and back-office systems with the up-front call processing functions of a call center. For example, agents can click on the dial function in a customer's record and CRM will automatically dial the customer's phone number. A broader example of the CRM concept is the multimedia call center server described in this book.

CTI

See computer telephony integration.

CTI link

The physical connection between a phone system and the PC or server, usually a serial cable or Ethernet LAN cable.

D

database hooking

The process whereby an automated system, such as a phone system, is able to request and retrieve meaningful information about callers from a database, which is then used to deliver a call through the call center system. The available data may be based on digits entered by the customer or ANI.

dedicated long distance

Your carrier usually provides this service over a T1 line. It is "dedicated" because the T1 is a direct connection between the carrier and customer that totally bypasses the local telephone company. The line is devoted solely to long-distance calling.

dialed number identification service (DNIS)

In essence, this is DID service via a dedicated telephone line. DNIS permits a carrier to assign its business customers multiple toll-free numbers over long-distance (T1) circuits. With a properly equipped phone system, a business can determine which toll-free number was dialed by its customer even before the phone system decides where to route the call.

DID

See direct inward dial.

DID trunk

These are the telephone lines, both analog and digital, used to provide DID service. An analog DID trunk is capable of carrying inbound calls only. When provided as channels on a local T1, DID trunks can be used for both inbound and outbound calls if so programmed.

digital (telephone signaling)

This method of transmitting telephone calls and other telecommunications signals is accomplished by converting the information to a digital format—ones (1s) and zeros (0s). Digital signaling is used in the backbones of telephone networks; in carrier service lines, such as T1; and in customer premises equipment, such as digital PBX and digital telephones.

digital subscriber line (DSL)

Local telephone companies use their existing copper infrastructure to offer this type of digital telephone line. Because it has been especially conditioned for use as a computer connection, DSL lines are often used to provide high-speed Internet connectivity, achieving much faster transmission rates than a standard 56 kbps dial-up modem. However, the distance between the carrier's central office and the subscriber determines the actual speed of a DSL line.

direct inward dial (DID)

By taking advantage of this telecommunications service, customers can obtain a disproportionate ratio of telephone numbers to the actual lines running into their businesses.

For example, with only four DID lines to carry calls on, a company could still provide individual numbers for each of its 25 employees. When any one of the company's numbers is dialed, the carrier transmits a signal to the phone system along with the call that indicates which number was dialed. The phone system then interprets the DID signal to route the incoming call to its correct destination within the company.

Divestiture Act of 1983

This piece of government legislation forced the breakup of the Bell telephone system's monopoly into seven regional Bell operating companies (RBOCs), which became the local phone companies, and AT&T, which was made up of Bell's long distance and telephone equipment divisions. The RBOCs were restricted to doing business within certain geographic boundaries, but the market for long-distance telephone service was open to all competition.

DNIS

See dialed number identification service.

DSL

See digital subscriber line.

DTMF

See dual tone multifrequency.

dual tone multifrequency (DTMF)

You are familiar with this technology by the name of Touch-Tone, an AT&T trademark. Each button you press on a telephone keypad emits a tone that consists of a combination of two frequencies—one high and one low. Hence, the name dual tone multifrequency.

Unlike dial pulses, DTMF signals pass through the entire telephone connection to the destination user. For this reason, DTMF lends itself to various schemes for remote control access after the connection is established, such as interactive voice response. Telephones using DTMF usually have 12 keys, each corresponding to a different pair of frequencies.

E

E & M (ear & mouth) circuit

The type of telephone line used to deliver services such as DID, tie lines, or foreign exchange lines.

F

FCC

See Federal Communications Commission.

Federal Communications Commission (FCC)

The government agency responsible for developing and enforcing federal regulation of the telecommunications industry.

foreign exchange (FX) line

Businesses may request a telephone number that originates in a local calling area other than its own. These "foreign" exchanges are similar to the toll-free numbers provided by long-distance carriers. Out-of-town customers can dial the business on its local number and thus avoid intra-LATA toll charges.

frame relay

This data circuit is used to create networks that join the computer systems of multiple offices together, or it may be used to create connections to other networks, such as the Internet. Frame relay resembles a private-line data service because it provides a link between two points. An important difference, however, is that frame relay utilizes a packet-based protocol over a *shared* network, meaning that users can access only a certain portion of a circuit's bandwidth.

For example, a business might order a 256 kbps circuit with a committed information rate (guarantee) of just 128 kbps. In this case, data transmissions bursting above 128 kbps may pass through the circuit, but only if the extra bandwidth is available on the frame relay network at that moment. This combination of oversubscription and packet-based switching allows carriers to sell frame relay service at a much lower cost than a dedicated circuit.

FX line

See foreign exchange line.

G

ground start trunk

These lines are similar to CO lines except for the technical protocol used to initiate a call on the line. Before a call can be dialed, the CO must be somehow triggered to provide a dial tone. Standard CO lines use the variations in loop current to initiate and tear down calls, while ground start trunks establish a ground on the line.

H

hold music

Most telephone systems are equipped to play music for customers to listen to while they are on hold. The source is typically provided by the phone system's owner, but there are also companies that will provide copyrighted music and audio programs for broadcasting over your business telephone system. Some can even create "hype-on-hold" programs, which blend music with advertising that features your business.

hunt group

See hunting. A group of telephone lines designated by a particular business that can be accessed via hunting. Other lines within the business will be excluded from the hunting process.

hunting

Many businesses have a group of telephone lines that are tied to a single main number. When a caller dials into the main number, the CO can be programmed to roll the call to each of the company's phone lines until it finds an open one. This service is known as hunting, and the order in which the lines are tried is called the hunting sequence.

Circular hunting rolls the call from the last line in the group back to the first line, while terminal hunting stops at the last line. The same hunting concept may also be applied to groups of extensions within a phone system.

hybrid telephone system

These mid-size business telephone systems typically offer more capabilities than a key telephone system, such as greater capacity or digital trunking capability (T1, DID, and so on).

I

ILEC
See incumbent local exchange carrier.

incumbent local exchange carrier (ILEC)
After the Telecom Reform Act of 1996 took effect, there was a need to differentiate between the established local phone companies and their competitors. Companies newly entering the market became known as competitive local exchange carriers (CLECs), while the established telcos were tagged as incumbents, or ILECs.

integrated services digital network (ISDN)
Your local phone company offers this digital service. Using a protocol that divides the circuit into multiple channels, ISDN accommodates either voice or data communications. There are two types of ISDN service—basic rate interface (BRI) and primary rate interface (PRI).

BRI provides one control channel for signaling information and two bearer channels for carrying data or telephone calls. PRI is a channelized T1 circuit that consists of a carrier channel and 23 bearer channels for voice or data. An important feature of ISDN is its capacity to create large data pipes when needed by bonding single (64 kbps) channels together. Such pipes are useful for certain types of high-volume data sessions, such as videoconference calls or Internet connections.

interactive voice response (IVR) system/server
These telephony servers allow callers to access a business database through a Touch-Tone keypad. For example, many banks utilize an IVR system so that customers can dial in to check account balances or other information. Callers first follow voice prompts

to choose the menu items that pertain to their questions. Then, rather than displaying data on a computer screen, IVR uses a digitized voice to convey the desired information to the caller.

interconnect (equipment vendor)

In this book, interconnect refers to locally owned, mid-size vendors. These companies usually serve as dealers for various equipment manufacturers, as well as installing and maintaining all types of business telephone systems and peripheral equipment.

An interconnect may also provide other services, such as computers and networking equipment, data and voice cabling, and the resale of local or long-distance telephone services.

interexchange carrier (IXC)

In short, these carriers are your long-distance phone companies. After Bell's divestiture in 1983, local telephone companies were barred from carrying traffic across LATA boundaries. The business of carrying telephone calls between LATAs was left exclusively to long-distance carriers.

interflow

This is the point of termination for an ACD queue, where the call may be transferred to a new location, terminated, or routed to an answering system or service.

inter-LATA (interstate) calling

Toll calling within the United States that terminates *outside* the state or LATA from which the call originates. These calls are billed by your long-distance phone company.

intra-LATA (intrastate) calling

Toll calling that terminates *within* the state or LATA from which the call originates. These calls may be billed by either your local phone company or your long-distance phone company.

ISDN
See integrated services digital network.

IVR system
See interactive voice response system.

IXC
See interexchange carrier.

K

key telephone system
Most often found in smaller businesses, these systems are easily recognized by a line of buttons appearing on each telephone set, the so-called "key line appearance." Each button is linked to an individual telephone line that can be accessed directly.

For example, in a business that uses five lines and a key system, each telephone set would feature five buttons labeled Line 1, Line 2, and so on through Line 5. Contrast this arrangement with a PBX system, where all lines are typically accessed by pressing "9."

L

LATA (local access and transport area)
Under the terms of the Modification of Final Judgment (MFJ) that broke up AT&T, LATAs were defined as geographical areas that generally conformed to standard metropolitan and statistical areas (SMSAs). Within these areas, divested regional Bell operating company (RBOCs) were permitted to offer exchange telecommunications and exchange access services.

However, the RBOCs were prohibited from providing services that originate in one LATA and terminate in another (long distance). The MFJ stated that such long-distance services would be provided by interexchange carriers (IXCs).

LEC
See local exchange carrier.

listen-only mailbox
Mailboxes on some voice mail systems can be programmed to play a greeting only. These listen-only boxes are used to provide repetitive information to customers, such as directions to the business location or the schedule for upcoming shows.

local exchange carrier (LEC)
These are the local telephone companies that provide service within each LATA, including both regional Bell operating companies (RBOCs) and independent LECs. There are several hundred small, independent LECs that serve less populated rural areas. LECs can be further categorized as incumbent local exchange carriers (ILECs), established phone companies, and competitive local exchange carriers (CLECs).

loop current
This is the electrical current on a telephone line that carries an analog voice signal.

M

manufacturer direct (equipment vendor)
These suppliers or installers of telephone equipment may be either a wholly owned branch office or a subsidiary of a telecommunications system manufacturer.

message of the day

Businesses can record easy-to-change preambles (messages of the day) that will be played for callers before they are entered into a queue. This feature is useful for providing answers to common, repetitive questions. If a customer's question is answered by the preamble, he can simply hang up rather than wait for an available agent.

monitoring unit (system)

When installed on the phone lines of a call center, this hard-wired, stand-alone unit gives supervisors access to the conversations of their agents.

multimedia call center server

A telephony server capable of providing multiple call center functions, such as ACD-style queuing or integrating incoming faxes into agent queues. In some cases, Internet chat sessions, email, and outbound calls may also be provided.

multimedia queue

This term refers to the stack of interactions being held by a multimedia call center server for delivery to the center's agents. This queue might consist of a variety of interactions, such as voice calls, outbound calls, abandoned callbacks, emails, faxes, or Web chat sessions. Usually, it is represented visually in a software interface on each agent's PC monitor.

N

night ringing bell

Phone systems can be programmed to ring this chime device— *not* part of a telephone—whenever an incoming call is received. Originally, bells were used after normal business hours to signal those employees who do not necessarily work near a telephone, such as night stockers in a grocery store or security guards.

O

off-premise extension (OPX) line

A business may choose to run a telephone line directly to its remote office that can only be used for calls between the two. The remote location is dialed as an extension off the original telephone system, thus providing a hot line between the two locations.

OPX line

See off-premise extension line.

outsourcer/outsourcing

In this book, I am referring to a call center that can be hired to perform outbound campaigns or answer inbound calls on behalf of other businesses.

overflow

The point when an ACD system or multimedia call center server begins to look beyond the originally intended call destinations for alternative places to send a queued interaction.

P

packet switching

This method of transporting data over shared communications channels breaks the data up into small pieces, known as packets. Packet switching optimizes the use of network resources (bandwidth) because the channel is only occupied during the time the packet is being transmitted. By contrast, the regular telephone network uses circuit switching, which ties up an entire channel for the duration of any given communication, even if there is no immediate activity on the line.

Because individual packets can be sent and received in any order, packet-switched networks allow many users to share the same channel. Examples of packet-switched network protocols include ATM, frame relay, TCP/IP, and X.25. The Internet was the first public packet-switched network.

PBX
See private branch exchange telephone systems.

phantom extensions
In many phone systems, a telephone extension can be programmed that does not actually connect to a wired telephone.

port
This is the name used for a plug-in outlet on a telephony system or server. It is the point where physical connection is made to a telephone line, T1 line, telephone station, voice mail system, and so on.

POTS (plain old telephone service)
Composed of standard telephones, telephone lines, and access to the public switched network, this is the basic analog voice service we are all familiar with. Specifically, POTS refers to the local loop, which is the predominantly analog connection between an individual subscriber and the nearest central office.

The term POTS may be used to indicate a CO line, but it is typically used to distinguish the local analog phone network from newer, digital services, such as ISDN and DSL.

predictive dialer

These devices are used by outbound call centers to automatically dial telephone numbers from a preprogrammed list. Then, only answered calls are connected to call center agents.

primary rate interface (PRI)

This is the T1 version of ISDN. PRI provides one carrier channel for signaling and 23 bearer channels for carrying traffic. Because it is a conditioned, data-ready telephone line, multiples of bearer channels can be bonded together to establish one data call. For example, a 512 kbps call could be set up for videoconferencing equipment by using 8 channels of 64 kbps each.

private branch exchange (PBX) telephone systems

These business telephone systems are usually larger and more sophisticated than a key system or hybrid system. The PBX version of a manufacturer's line of telephone systems is usually the one with the highest processing capability and the one with the most sophisticated set of features and options.

The term private branch exchange is a throwback to the days when operators used cord boards to make the physical connections (exchanges) between telephone lines. If your business had enough telephones to require your own cord board or switching system, you were said to have a private branch exchange.

profiling

In the process of hiring new agents, call centers often measure each candidate's qualifications against an established profile that defines the ideal call center agent. Such profiling typically lists a predetermined set of skills, experiences, and capabilities deemed optimal for the position being filled.

PSTN
See public switched telephone network.

public switched telephone network (PSTN)
This global, landline telephone network is accessible to anyone with an active connection, who also pays the required access fee. The PSTN is made up mostly of analog local loops that connect subscribers to the local central office, but it also includes digital facilities that link central offices together via various regional, long-distance, and international backbones.

The PSTN is comprised of interconnecting networks owned by a multitude of service providers, including incumbent local exchange carriers (ILECs), competitive local exchange carriers (CLECs), and interexchange carriers (IXCs) in the U.S. In foreign countries, the networks may be privately owned or public monopoly telephone companies.

R

RAD
See recorded announcement device.

recorded announcement device (RAD)
Automated call processing systems use this device to play messages, such as the in-queue messages of an ACD system.

RBOC
See regional Bell operating company.

reader board (display board)
Most call centers post statistical information or messages on overhead digital displays for their agents to refer to. These display

boards change continuously as new data is fed in from the ACD or multimedia call center system.

refurbished (telecommunications equipment)
Used telephone equipment in good working order is frequently cleaned and resold by companies that specialize in this market.

regional Bell operating company (RBOC)
These are the seven original local telephone companies created from the divestiture of the Bell telephone system in 1983. The other entity created was the long-distance carrier AT&T.

S

screen pop
When an agent receives an incoming call, this technology simultaneously delivers the customer's record to the agent's desktop computer screen. The Screen pops are enabled by software plus caller ID or ANI (automatic number identification).

screen scraping
This software technique records a picture of the current appearance of a given PC monitor. The technology is mostly used to monitor agent performance via a customer assurance server. Screen scraping every fraction of a second or so allows each agent's interactions with a customers to be documented.

skills-based routing
In ACD or multimedia call center systems, this method for routing calls to agents is based on predetermined skill levels. The various levels will have been previously programmed into the system's software by a system administrator. Typically, skills-based routing will match callers to the appropriate agents

according to the prompt they choose at the beginning of the call (press "1" for product A; press "2" for product B, and so on).

SMDR
See station message detail recording/reporting.

station card
The printed circuit board located inside a business telephone system that physically connects telephone extensions to the system.

station message detail recording/reporting (SMDR)
Most business telephone systems either have, or can be equipped with, an output port that will post a record about every call made to or from the system. Information usually recorded includes the number dialed (on an outbound call) or the number dialing (on an inbound call for a phone system equipped to read ANI). The time, date, and duration of the call, plus the originating or terminating extension, are also typically recorded. When captured by call accounting systems, this raw data can provide a business with useful and relevant reports about telephone traffic and usage.

switched long distance
This term refers to service provided by a long-distance telephone company in conjunction with your regular local telephone lines. The local phone company switches your toll calls to a long-distance carrier for delivery to their destination.

switching matrix
Within a business telephone system, this is the circuitry that is responsible for establishing connections between stations (telephones and other devices) and telephone lines. The same

term could be applied to other types of equipment, such as data routers or central office switches, that make similar internal circuit connections.

T

T1

A single digital telephone circuit consisting of 24 channels of 64 kbps each. These channels are used by local phone companies to provide 24 lines of local phone service; by long-distance carriers to provide 24 dedicated connections to their networks; or by data carriers to provide up to 1.544 Mbps data pathways.

Each voice conversation requires only one 64 kbps channel, but any number of 64 kbps channels can be combined into a bigger pipe for data transmission. While a T1 line is the most basic and common carrier circuit, it used to provide many complex and advanced types of telecommunications services. These lines are widely used in all types of voice switches, business telephone systems, and data connectivity equipment.

T1 line card

Similar to a station card, this is the printed circuit board in a business telephone system (or switch) that physically connects a T1 circuit to the system.

TAPI

See telephony applications programming interface.

Telecom Reform Act of 1996

The net result of this legislative act was the deregulation of local telephone business. In exchange for opening their local markets to competition, incumbent local exchange carriers (ILECs) are now able to compete in the lucrative long-distance voice and data markets.

telemarketing
Businesses employing this marketing method use telephones almost exclusively to reach customers, usually in broad-based, mass appeals or sales campaigns.

telemarketing campaign
A planned telemarketing program developed and implemented by either a business or an outsourcer that identifies specific goals for the call center.

telephony applications programming interface (TAPI)
This software protocol was developed by Microsoft. It acts as an interface between specially equipped telephone systems and software applications that run under the Microsoft Windows family of personal computer operating systems.

telephony services applications programming interface (TSAPI)
Developed by Novell, this software protocol acts as an interface between specially equipped telephone systems and applications that run under Novell's family of computer network operating systems.

terminal hunting
In this method of hunting, the system tries a group of telephone lines or extensions in sequence, but terminates the hunt at the last number in the group. Customers calling into a busy terminal hunt group will receive a busy signal from the central office.

tie line
This term refers to any telecommunications circuit that provides a direct connection between two points. In business, private tie lines can be used to link together computer systems at two or more remote offices. In a carrier's network, tie lines are used to transport traffic between switching offices and network nodes.

tip & ring

These are the two sides of a two-wire analog telephone circuit. On one wire, the current flows into the telephone or device; on the other wire, the current flows back to the central office.

toll-free service

Customers can place toll calls to subscribers of this service from specified rate areas within the North American Numbering Plan (NANP) without incurring long-distance charges. Toll-free numbers now include 888, 877, 866, and 855 in addition to the well-known 800.

tree mailbox

This method of programming a voice mailbox presents callers with a menu of choices that typically branch off into other menus until the caller is successfully routed to his correct destination.

For example, a department routing mailbox might prompt you to press "1" for sales, "2" for accounting, and so on. If you chose sales, the next menu might ask you to press "1" to place an order, "2" to check on an order's status, "3" to speak to a personal shopper, and so forth. A tree mailbox does not record messages; it only provides routing.

trunk lines

This is a loose term that has been applied to many different telephone circuits. Carrier networks refer to tie lines and the connections to other carrier networks as trunk lines, and the connections between central offices are called trunk lines. At one time, the distinction between an interoffice trunk and a line to someone's house or business was important. Now that all switching is handled within sophisticated automatic switching equipment, the distinction is less relevant.

When connected to PBXs, both CO lines and the channels of T1 circuits are sometimes called trunk lines. Furthermore, "trunk" may be used to indicate a telephone line that connects to equipment rather than a standard telephone (such as your home phone).

trunk utilization reporting
This type of reporting is provided by some call accounting systems or it may be offered as a service by a local exchange carrier. Its purpose is to detail information about the activity of a group of telephone lines. Companies commonly use these reports to determine how many times all their phone lines were in use at the same time during the month. This information will tell them how often their customers are receiving busy signals.

trunker (equipment vendor)
These small companies typically consist of one or two people selling business telephone systems and service, often without benefit of a physical business office. Traditionally, they are said to work from the trunk of their cars; hence, "trunkers."

TSAPI
See telephony services applications programming interface.

T-span
Another name for a T1 line.

U

UCD
See universal/uniform call distribution.

unified messaging (server)

This voice mail system takes advantage of computer telephony integration to provide its users with access to voice mail, email, and sometimes fax. from Common computer interfaces are employed, such as Microsoft's Outlook or Lotus Notes, both email programs. Most unified systems also permit access to the various message media they support through a traditional voice mail telephone interface.

universal/uniform call distribution

When programmed into a business telephone system, this technology distributes calls among a group of stations.

V

voice mail

A computerized system that can play and record messages and greetings.

voice over IP (Internet Protocol)

To transmit telephone (voice) traffic across data networks, the application of several technologies is required—Internet Protocol (IP), packet switching, and digital telecommunications transmission.

W

wall board

See reader board.

Web callback requests

Some multimedia call center servers permit customers to request a callback via a website interface.

Web chat

Using a keyboard and text, two individuals can communicate back and forth in real time over the Internet. In many ways, chat sessions resemble two-way radio communications, only in text form.

Call centers encourage customers browsing the Internet to communicate with their agents online rather than calling on the phone. Many times, a customer's active Internet connection is his only phone line. Businesses using Web chat can minimize the possibility of losing the customer who must log off to make a phone call.

white noise

Some call centers pump low-volume static through a sound system in their facilities to help agents reduce stress. The theory is that as agents unconsciously filter out the white noise, any background noise at or below the same volume level will be filtered out as well.

Index

M

MCI 50
measured business line 53
Microwave Communications,
    Inc.. *See* MCI
monitoring 193

N

Needle Food Corporation 175
needs analysis 252
Novell 167
Nynex 51

O

off-premise extension 68
OPX. *See* off-premise
    extension
outsourcer 87
outsourcing 214
overflow 109

P

Pacific Bell 51
packet switching 69
path 107
PBX telephone system 33
PCmusician 147
performance goals 233
plain old telephone service 53
POTS. *See* plain old telephone
    service
predictive dialer 81
PRI. *See* primary rate interface
primary rate interface 62
private branch exchange. *See*
    PBX telephone system
purchasing process 250

Q

queue 107

R

RBOC. *See* regional Bell
    operating company
Read, Brendan B. 230
regional Bell operating
    company 51

S

salary 225
screen pop 22
screen scraping 200
Seattle This Week 38
signaling
    dial pulse 54
    digital 57, 61
skills-based routing 106
SMDR. *See* station message
    detail reporting
Southwestern Bell 51
space planner 220
staffing service 231
station message detail
    reporting 204
Stephen A. Laser Associates
    230
Subscription Technicians 82

T

T1 service 56
Talent+ 230
TAPI. *See* telephony
    applications programming
    interface
TDM. *See* time-division
    multiplexing
Telecom Reform Act 52